Handmade Home

Handmade Home

Simple Ways to Repurpose Old Materials into New Family Treasures

AMANDA BLAKE SOULE

Trumpeter
Boston & London
2009

TRUMPETER BOOKS
An imprint of Shambhala Publications, Inc.
Horticultural Hall
300 Massachusetts Avenue
Boston, Massachusetts 02115
www.shambhala.com

9 8 7 6 5 4 3 2

Printed in the United States of America

⊗ This edition is printed on acid-free paper that meets the American
National Standards Institute Z39.48 Standard.
♻ This book was printed on 30% postconsumer recycled paper.
For more information please visit www.shambhala.com.

Distributed in the United States by Random House, Inc.,
and in Canada by Random House of Canada Ltd

Designed by Lora Zorian

LIBRARY OF CONGRESS CATALOGING-IN-PUBLICATION DATA
Soule, Amanda Blake.
Handmade home: simple ways to repurpose old materials
into new family treasures / Amanda Blake Soule.—1st ed.
p. cm.
ISBN 978-1-59030-595-9
1. Handicraft. I. Title.
TT157.S6365 2009
745.5—dc22
2008045457

Dedicated to my foremothers, all "makers" of beauty

Florence, Dorothy, Millie, Edrie

*To be surrounded by beautiful things
has much influence upon the human creature;
to make beautiful things has more.*

—Charlotte Perkins Gilman

Contents

Acknowledgments

My deepest thanks to:

Everyone at Trumpeter Books, who have made the process of making books a true pleasure and honor for me to be a part of.

Jennifer Brown, for the wise, encouraging, and thoughtful way in which she edited and guided this project.

Linda Roghaar, my agent, for her invaluable advice and guidance along the way.

Amy Karol, Alicia Paulson, Anna Maria Horner, and Ali Edwards, for the inspiration, experience and friendship they have shared.

Meg Rooks, Stacy Brenner and my sister Michelle Ames, for sharing their stories, crafts, newborn babies and all manner of other loveliness for this book.

The readers of SouleMama for their support and kindness each day and through the years. Thank you for helping to make so many wonderful things possible!

My family—both the one I was born in and the one I was so blessed to marry into—for passing on a love of family history, tradition, and old-fashioned Yankee DIY that is both in my heart and at the heart of this book.

My dearest girlfriends Rachael, Jessie, Jean, and Brandie. Words can't express what you mean to me, or the many ways you have contributed to this book—thank you, and I love you.

And my deepest gratitude and love to the ones with whom I am so honored to share my "everyday" with—my partners in every way, in all that I do—Harper, Adelaide, Ezra, Calvin, and Steve. Thanks for keeping me on the path and sharing it with me, my loves.

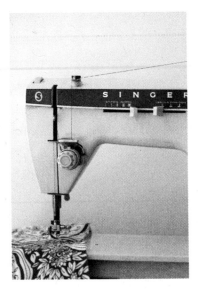

Introduction

Each day provides us with the opportunity to create something. *What can we make today?* It's a question I love to hear from my little ones, and it's a question in my own heart each and every day. Making things by hand is a way I share my love and a bit of myself with those dearest to me. Whether it be diapers to clothe my soon-to-be-born babe, blankets to keep us all warm on cool winter nights, or a special handbag for a mama's night out, each time I make something for my home and my family, I feel a satisfaction unlike any other feeling. I find such joy in gathering what's around me, dreaming and stitching it into something new, and putting it to use in the hands of those I love.

Through the act of making I find solace and peace in the small moments of my everyday life. When I am at work making things, I am fully present in the moment as I breathe new life into something, while at the very same time, I am fulfilling a need or a desire for my family. I am reminded rather symbolically that we can only do one stitch at a time, and therefore one step at a time and one breath at a time in this life. Mending, sewing, and creating provide us with a beautiful opportunity to stop running and to relish a small moment in time as we go about our task. When I sit to sew, I am fully aware of the sound of the needle coming in and out through my linen, and that quickly becomes the background—the heartbeat—to the other sounds in my life, the sounds of my children playing, the music of our days. I try, then, to carry this rhythm with me through my days and my world. When making things, I am not thinking about what happened or what is yet to come. I am fully aware of what is happening *now*.

Most all of the things I make are for my family and our family home. Home, as our primary place of comfort, nourishment, love, and soul. Home is our place of peace and comfort both for us and for our children. Filling my home with items I've made by hand—that have, in effect, been infused with love in their making—is one of the ways I show those closest to me how very much I love them. Sprinkling some handmade creations through our home makes it a truly unique representation of who we are. Looking around at the things in our home, I can see who we are, what we value, and how we spend our time. These furnishings become comfort, peace, and the landscape in which our family grows, learns, and loves together.

Much of the making I do blends my love of creating with my love of old things and my desire to use what we have. Repurposing (the act of making something new from something old) is an important part of creating for me. We need only look a few generations back to find people who out of necessity were able to make new things from old, people who had an ability to see a second life in something once its first purpose was finished. Like most women of her generation, my great grandmother Florence—"Grammie Gile" to me, though we never met—would buy fabric to make her clothes herself and later turn them into clothing for her children. When the clothes no longer fit the children, they were deconstructed and remade into dolls' clothing and toys. Ultimately they ended up as quilts and rugs and rags. Things were truly "worn" until they could be no longer. My mother tells of visiting my Grammie Gile and of the treasured bucket of empty wooden spools that all the grandchildren used as building blocks and of the paper dolls that they made together out of old Sears catalogs. Nothing was wasted, and nothing was simply tossed aside. When clothing was deconstructed, every button and snap was saved and used over and over again until it could be used no longer. "Waste not, want not," my grandmother—Grammie Gile's daughter—would say to me years later as she snipped the buttons off her own old and worn clothing. If we don't waste what we have now, we will not need later.

My family is full of stories such as these, and I'm sure yours is, too. Resourcefulness was simply a fact and necessity of home life for many generations before ours. And while a few generations of consumerism and a disposable living have come to pass in recent years, many of us today are finding our way home to this more back-to-basics resourcefulness. Today, I'm drawn to repurposing for so many reasons: It allows me to live a more financially pared-down and simple life in which

it's possible to work a little bit less and live a little bit more. It allows me to connect to the past and preserve a more traditional way of life. It allows me to place value on the work of the hands and the value of human time, energy, art, and craft. It allows me an aesthetic and a quality of materials that are increasingly harder to find in today's quick and disposable products. It allows me to lessen my family's impact on the very earth we are so blessed to live upon. Marrying such values as these with my craft is such a joy for me. Not only do I feel the peace and solace in making things, but I also feel good about being able to reflect my lifestyle choices and values in my crafts.

As a crafter, I'm always looking for the next thing I want to make. As a mama, I'm always looking for the next thing we need—to do, to have, to use—as a family. The coming together of these parts is where the heart of *Handmade Home* lies. In this book you'll find a range of projects—from picnic blankets made out of repurposed bedsheets to curtains made out of vintage handkerchiefs—that express this sense of making something new out of something old. For me, when I finish one of these projects, I not only feel a sense of accomplishment for having completed a project, but I also have a feeling of saving something that might otherwise have had a long and drawn-out fate in a landfill. It matters not that the thing I've made or mended may be small, but it matters greatly that it gave me a moment of peace and a sense of accomplishment in my day. It is not, by any means, a mended sock to bring about world peace and stop global warming, but it is a mended sock to bring me peace in my everyday, to lessen the amount of waste that my family contributes to the earth we love so dearly, and to warm the hearts and toes of my children.

I believe this must have been how women before me felt in their own day-to-day lives. With poverty, hardship, and tragedy all around them, maybe they found a similar sense of comfort and accomplishment in these seemingly small and mundane tasks, tasks that may very well have soothed their souls. While we can look to these women of our past with respect and admiration, we can also be grateful for the present day in which we have the beautiful ability to choose—to choose how we spend our money, what we consume, how we spend our time, and what earthly resources we use. We can thank the women before us who fought to ensure that domesticity was a choice and not something required of all women. Thanks be to them that these

expectations are no longer required of us but are now an option among many that we may choose if we so wish. Free from the burden of expectation, we can now look to domestic arts and skills to create and express ourselves in our homes, giving full respect to the art and skill they encompass.

Blessed by both the history and materials of generations past together with our modern knowledge, awareness, and options, we have a beautiful opportunity at this point in time to make a change in our lives. In a world of increasingly limited earthly resources, it is true that all of our decisions—small and large—have a powerful impact. Our small actions can improve not only our earth, but also our hearts, our spirits, and our children—and bring about the kind of change that is the most powerful, the most heartfelt, and the most personal. Our role in living a greener life for our children and ourselves can begin to reverse some of the damage we have done to the earth and provide a bit of healing for it and ourselves, while at the very same time, providing a home life that is richer in heart, soul, history, and hope for the future. If it is true that peace begins at home, as I believe it does, this change might even reach beyond the walls of our family homes.

It is my grandest of hopes that the ideas in this book will help you in small, but powerful ways to deepen the role of home in your family life; that the projects in this book will encourage us all to be a little more mindful of the fleeting and beautiful moments of family life; and that all of us—and our earth—may flourish with just a little more soul in our hearts and homes.

Getting started

Repurposing Fabrics

~~~~~~~~~~

The first fabrics I ever sewed with belonged to my grandmother. They were bright, bold, slightly psychedelic prints from the 1960s, and I loved them. I loved that they were unique, that they had a history to them, and that I was giving them new life by saving them from the fate of sitting on the fabric shelves—or worse, in a landfill—for more decades to come.

Ever since then, I've felt drawn to working with vintage fabrics. Sometimes a certain print evokes strong memories of my own childhood, like a Vera pillowcase I remember from visits to my grandmother's house or a corduroy I'm sure I wore as handmade pants in the '70s. Other times a vintage fabric evokes not a specific memory but a feeling of another time and another era. The feedsack prints of the '20s and '30s, for example, remind me of families living simpler lives when more time was spent together—and more time was spent making things themselves.

For all of these reasons and more, I find myself looking for and using vintage materials to create the things I treasure most for my family and my home. I choose old materials that are readily and affordably available to me and sometimes combine them with the new—either in the form of contemporary fabrics or modern design.

The projects in this book use old materials in new ways, and through making these projects, you will learn to view the ordinary in new and creative ways. Many of these old materials may be hidden away in your own home. Your attic, basement, and linen closet might be full of fabrics just waiting to have a little bit of new life breathed into them. There's also grandma's attic, your friend's cast-offs from spring cleaning, or an online swap or auction site where you can find just what you're looking for. Thrift shops, charity centers, yard sales, rummage sales, and flea markets are often overflowing with useful materials. There are so many places around us where these materials can be found, claimed, and remade. Keep your eyes open, never take more than you need or have room for, and let your mind imagine how you can repurpose what you see around you.

Choosing Vintage Fabrics

Once you begin to look, you'll find materials everywhere to repurpose. But how do you select fabrics? What should you be looking for? Mostly, your choices are a matter of personal taste. Bring home fabrics that you are drawn to, that you love, that fit your taste and style, and that you can see yourself using. You may find yourself intrigued by a color, a texture, a certain design or style, or just that certain special *something*.

Beyond personal taste, the condition of the original piece is important to note. Pristine fabrics are ideal, but just because a piece is soiled, torn, or worn does not necessarily mean it's unusable. The beauty of working with vintage fabrics often lies in the very elements of wear and age. Fade spots may work well in your creations, giving them an antique and loved look, and many stains can be removed with the proper treatment.

Some of the most affordable pieces of vintage fabric can be found as "cutters," which means that the pieces contain stains, rips, or tears, making them suitable only after some sections have been cut away. When viewing a less-than-perfect piece of fabric, ask yourself the following questions:

1. Can it be cleaned?
2. Can the damaged part be removed?
3. Will I still have enough fabric to work with?

If the answers are yes, then the fabric is yours! As you can see, extending the life of a textile means getting a little creative in how you first view it.

Another consideration when choosing vintage fabric is the material itself. Is it cotton or another natural fiber, such as linen? Fabrics made from natural fibers are preferred for most of the projects in this book. While fabrics with a high polyester content could be used, they will not work as well with your home sewing machine and the finished project may not feel so fabulous against your skin. My suggestion is to leave that mod polyester leisure suit fabric behind and focus instead on cotton dresses, wool jackets, and other natural fiber finds.

Preparing and Storing Your Fabrics

Once you've purchased or found fabric pieces to bring home, cleaning and storing them should be your next priority. It is essential that you clean the fabric before you store it on your shelves. This step can avoid further staining, keep odors from emanating and spreading, destroy wool moths, and prevent many more sad fabric tales.

Begin by removing any pieces of the fabric that are too torn, too stained, or otherwise unusable.

Next, choose your washing method. Most cottons can be machine washed. If you have doubts, wash them on a gentle cycle. More delicate things—doilies, lace, very old cotton fabric, and quilts—should be washed by hand. First soak them overnight in cool water with a mild soap. The following morning, gently squeeze the fabric to remove excess water and hang the item on a line or lay it flat to dry.

After washing, decide if you need additional stain removal for stubborn spots. Carefully consider the type of stain and the type of fabric before employing any stain removal techniques. Vintage fabric can easily be ruined by aggressive measures.

When your fabric is clean and dry, press it to iron out any wrinkles and to keep the fabric lying flat while it's in storage.

Depending on your work and available space, any number of storage solutions—from open shelving to suitcases to plastic storage bins—may work for you. Be sure to store your fabric away from extreme temperature changes and bright sun. Check your stash periodically (especially wool) for the appearance of moths.

Vintage Materials

Vintage materials aren't limited to just fabrics. Following is a comprehensive list of potential materials to be used in projects in this book. Some might be found right in your own home; others might be found while you are out thrifting.

LIGHTWEIGHT TO MIDWEIGHT FABRICS

any cotton fabric
feedsacks
pillowcases
flannel bed sheets
cotton bed sheets
linens
doilies
handkerchiefs

tablecloths
silk scarves
flannel shirts
T-shirts
jersey baby blankets

MIDWEIGHT TO HEAVYWEIGHT FABRICS

upholstery fabric
canvas fabric
coverlets
bedspreads
wool blankets
quilts
towels
curtains
fabric shower curtains
wool sweaters
wool suits
corduroy clothing

OTHER MATERIALS

webbed belts
children's books
hardwood scraps
window screen

Finding Vintage
and Thrifted Materials

~~~~~~~~~

There is enough on earth for everybody's need,
but not for everyone's greed.

—Mahatma Gandhi

Where do you find repurposed fabrics? By thrifting! As a child, my grandmother and I would spend summer days traveling from road to road in rural Maine searching for yard sales, garage sales, and antique barns. I would always return home with at least one little treasure. Our mission was that of fun and adventure, entirely. But since then, as I've continued to thrift throughout my life, I've discovered many reasons why thrifting makes good sense: politics, nostalgia, economics, and perhaps most of all, the environment. More and more people are thrifting as a way to lessen their impact on the earth. And along the way, they're getting quality goods with a connection to the past.

I've had some wonderful finds over the years—some practical and some entirely for fun. Surely there is some luck and good fortune involved, but I also think successful thrifters need some skills. Whether you're a seasoned thrifter yourself or just getting your feet wet for the first time, I hope you'll find some ideas and tips here that will make your thrifting time well spent, and most important of all, fun!

Where to Go

Note: Throughout this book, for brevity's sake, I've used the word "thrifting" to refer to all of the following methods of finding things.

Yard Sales and Garage Sales

While the popularity of yard and garage sales may vary a bit regionally, in the spring, summer, and fall months in Maine, weekends are full of these events, mostly on Saturdays, but often on Fridays and Sundays as well. You might stumble upon a few as you're driving through town, but the most efficient way to locate sales is to check your newspaper's classified section. There you'll find listings of yard sales, broken down by city or neighborhood. Before I spend a Saturday morning yard "sailing," I clip Friday's garage sale section of the classifieds, circle a few locations that sound interesting to me, and plot my course. Mapping a route may seem over the top, but it truly saves time and gas. Because really, all that carbon dioxide you'd be releasing isn't exactly worth a few yards of vintage fabric is it? Better yet, plan to thrift with friends—it's more fun, and it cuts the driving even more. Be sure to put any neighborhood or group sales first on your list so you can spend more time sailing in less space.

In the morning, I rise and shine early, grab some coffee, and head out the door. I try to arrive at the first sales when they open by 7 or 8 A.M., and stay out for just a few hours. The best treasures are to be found first thing in the morning, and then I still have the rest of my day for other things.

At yard sales, you're generally dealing with people just like you—not dealers, not sellers. Yard sale organizers are families, just like your own, who might just be looking to clean out a bit and make a little money along the way. With this in mind, it's essential to play by the rules and be nice. Thrifting karma is very important.

- *The early bird gets the worm.* Oh, so true for yard sailing! Arriving right at the opening time is fine, but please don't show up early—unless you've been invited to do so (some advertisements will say "Early Birds Welcome"). Remember that these people have likely been up before the sun to haul treasures out of their basements and garages. They need time to get ready. Give them a break and show up at the time they asked you to.
- *Bring small bills.* Even the most prepared of sellers will be hard pressed to give you change for that twenty-dollar bill when your item costs fifty cents. Bring small bills, and some change, too. It's easier for everyone.
- *Haggle, but not always.* It's perfectly fine to haggle—to ask for a lower price—at yard sales. I do so often. But be sure that you're haggling because you really believe the item is worth less or you need it for less. Don't haggle just for the sake of haggling.
- *Say "Thank you."* Seriously. Even if you don't buy anything, just give a thank you on your way out. Laying all their stuff out for people to peruse can leave a family feeling a bit vulnerable, let alone exhausted, from all the work. If they've been dealing with aggressive dealers and haggling customers all morning, a well-meant thank-you will be very welcome.

Flea Markets and Antique Malls

If you're looking for vintage items, in particular, and are willing to pay for the convenience of finding more of what you're looking for in a shorter period of time in smaller location, then the flea markets are for you. Flea markets and antique malls are generally a set of stalls—inside or out, permanent or temporary—run by antique dealers and sellers. Often they'll carry specific items, so it isn't uncommon to find tables full of just vintage fabrics or just linens (or tables full of vintage Pyrex for that matter). More bang for your buck, so to speak, than at yard sales.

The trade-off is that the prices are usually a bit higher. With the prevalence of online auction sites, every good seller at today's flea markets and antique malls knows what he or she has and how much it could sell for online, and that variable has been factored into the pricing—for better or worse. It is OK to haggle with most flea market sellers. Feel out the situation. With some experience, you'll be able to tell who's up for making a deal.

Thrift Shops

Ah, the things you can find at the thrift shop. Ninety-five percent of my family's wardrobe comes from the thrift shop. The same could be said for our furniture, dishes, and on and on. Scouring the thrift shops for that many items can take some dedication. I usually visit a thrift shop once a week, and leave just as often with nothing as I do with bags full.

Thrift shops are generally run by nonprofit organizations, such as a church or social organization. Ask around in your area for favorite thrift shops, and you'll find out which ones are the best bets for what you're seeking. If you go often enough and keep your ears open, you'll find out when they get new shipments in or when it's half-price day—all important considerations for getting what you need at a bargain price.

Rummage Sales

The church rummage sale is my favorite place to visit for old-fashioned bargains. In my experience, New England churches in particular generally have big rummage sales as a fund-raiser in either the spring or fall months, as well as sometimes at their holiday fairs. You'll usually see rummage sales listed in the classified section of the newspaper along with the yard sales, or you'll spot signs in front of the church itself.

What you find at a church rummage sale can really vary from sale to sale, but once you find one you like, you'll be mentally marking it in your calendar for years to come. Prices vary, but the variety is often very good. The ones I visit regularly are my favorite sources for vintage linens, fabrics, and dishes. Church rummage sales are also my favorite places for gathering the stories that go along with the treasures. Many church sales are run by the elderly women and men in the church community who may surprise you with a lovely tale or two.

Thrifting with Children

I will admit that most of my yard sailing, antiquing, and rummaging takes place without my children. I'm more mobile that way, it's easier to move around in a crowd, and it's a chance for a little bit of alone "mama thinking time," as my six-year-old calls it. However, I do take my children to the thrift shop with me often, and I have found a few things that make the experience more pleasant for the kids, myself, and everyone else in the store.

- *Be sure that children are well fed and well rested.* I know this is common sense, but I will admit to pushing past these things a few times to make a quick stop somewhere. It never goes well. Lesson learned: be sure everyone's happy before you go in.
- *If it's OK with the shop, bring a little snack.* For us, this means that two of the three get in the cart, and they share a bag of pretzels and bottled water. It's easy, not messy, and keeps them fed and happy for a few moments.
- *Include them.* Talk before you go in about what it is that you're looking for, if anything in particular. Ask if there's anything they're looking for, and look for it. Including them not only keeps them happy in the process of shopping, but it's also teaching them some valuable lessons along the way. If they're old enough, include them in the handling of the money or encourage them to bring their own. Learning about spending money in a thrift shop versus a store full of new expensive things is a wonderful way for them to learn the value of a dollar.
- *Buy a book.* In my experience, it is easier to find a quality children's book at a thrift store than a quality toy I would want in our home, and so we established the one book rule early on in our family thrifting career. Everyone gets one book of their choosing (with, um, a few parental vetoes allowed; the 1940s *Boys Guide to Gun Hobbies* didn't come home with us). Often they'll spend the time in the shop either looking for their book or reading the ones they've chosen.

What to Look For

Why, anything you need, of course! Be careful to buy only what you have a need, a use, or a desire for. It's too easy to get caught up in, "But it's such a great deal!" when you're buying secondhand. It's not such a great deal when it ends up serving as clutter in your home or mind. If the item you're considering purchasing is not something you really love or actually need and will use, then it's best to leave that deal behind for another thrifter who actually can use it. Think of it as feeding the thrifting karma again.

If you're easily tempted—as we all are at times— you might find it helpful to have an ongoing list in mind while thrifting. Try carrying a written list to help you stay on task and remember the specific things you are hoping to find. Write down the sizes of family members' clothing and shoes (I find this last bit particularly helpful, as I have a hard time remembering the changing shoe sizes, for example, for the five people in my family). Sometimes my list includes items like size 12 rain boots, rollerblades for Calvin, umbrella for kids' play, more Pyrex bowls (there's always room for a few more vintage Pyrex bowls in my house), square coffee table, or winter jacket for Steve. I also believe that a bit of "write it down and it will happen" occurs when these lists are made. You never know what you might find and when!

Finding Thrifted Sewing Tools and Notions

In addition to finding fabric for your projects while out thrifting, also keep your eye out for the other materials you may need. Sewing machines, tools, and most notions can be found used, vintage, or secondhand. These bargain finds not only add a little bit of retro to your work, but they'll also save you a bit of money in your creative projects. Watch for the following sewing-related items when you are out thrifting.

Sewing Machines

If you are just beginning to sew and are looking for a machine, buy only what you need. A new basic sewing machine will cost a few hundred dollars or less. Go with a brand name that you recognize and trust. All new machines will have the two basic stitches you need to get started: straight and zigzag. New sewing machines can be found at most department stores and at specialty sewing shops. While you may end up spending slightly more, the benefit to buying a machine from a local fabric shop is that you can usually test out the models to find the perfect machine for you. You can also talk with a knowledgeable staff person. Some shops will also offer trade-ins, so upgrading your original machine for the next best model becomes a possibility later on.

You may also want to consider using an older machine. It's quite likely that your mother—or your grandmother—might have a sewing machine that she doesn't use anymore. In addition to the fabulous retro aspect of an older machine, there's also a sturdy reliability. If you find an older machine at a thrift shop, it's likely to be quite inexpensive. You can get yourself a funky-looking machine while extending its life.

If you decide to go with an older machine, keep the following in mind.

Be sure you have the manual. Always try to get a sewing machine with the manual still included. That little book will be really helpful as all machines are different. Sometimes, you can find the manual online, so check there as well.

Have the machine serviced before using it. Any machine that's been sitting around for a while will need a tune-up, and it will be nice to have a professional take a look at the machine and offer you some information about that particular brand and model.

Sewing Notions

At your local thrift shop, flea market, or antique store you can often find older sewing notions. Many of them are perfectly suited to using today, and they can be a very economical and eco-friendly way to build your sewing stash. Some sewing notions to look out for when thrifting include the following:

rick rack
needles
bias tape
batting (preferably cotton)
embroidery floss
embroidery hoops
elastic
sewing and knitting patterns
knitting needles and crochet hooks
spools of thread
zippers

ON BUYING WOOD

Buying reclaimed or salvaged wood not only has aesthetic benefits, but it also has environmental benefits as well. Try the following places to look for wood for the projects in this book:

- salvage companies that reclaim timber and wood
- ads in your local paper
- transfer stations, dumps, and dumpsters (provided, of course, that it's legal for you to do so!)
- www.freecycle.com
- www.salvegeweb.com

preparing to sew

~~~~~~~~~~

Take your needle, my child, and work at your pattern—
it will come out a rose by and by. Life is like that . . .
one stitch at a time, taken patiently.

—OLIVER WENDELL HOLMES

This section is by no means intended to provide you with a complete guide to sewing. In fact, you will not find any sewing how-to here. There are plenty of wonderful resources out there for learning how to sew (some are listed in the resources at the end of this book). Instead, I hope this section will give you a few things to help you get started, as well as cover the materials needed throughout the book.

As a beginning sewer, there is no need to fall into the trap of buying all the materials and all the sewing tools and gadgets available—and there are many. There is no need to rush out and stock a studio full of tools and big machines yet. Wait and see how much time you will spend sewing, look for the materials that you will use, and buy things only as you need them.

Setting Up a Space for Sewing

Of course it's lovely when we're able to dedicate an entire room—or part of a room—to our sewing. If you have that available to you, then I'm sure you need no help from me in setting it up. My guess is that you're well on your way to piles of fabric and notions and sewing goodness! But many of us are sewing in areas that double for other purposes in our house—a corner in a bedroom, a sun porch, the dining room table!

The dining room table is where I spent several years of sewing time, and while it can be a bit tricky to manage, it is definitely doable. Admittedly, cleaning off the dining room table each night from the day's sewing projects sometimes became a hassle, but I did love that my creative time was spent with my family so close by. My children could see me sewing, and I was able to go back and forth between sewing and playing and housework. The fluidity felt quite natural and lovely most of the time.

My Nana tells of bringing her sewing machine to the dining table each night after she put her children to bed. There she would stay up until the wee hours of the morning, making clothing for herself and her five children—both out of necessity and pleasure. She'd clean the table off, get some sleep, and be back at the table for breakfast several hours later. For her, the dining room table was a central spot for living and playing and work.

Here are some tips for sewing when you're short on space:

- If you use a small table in a corner of a room, use a sewing machine cover/cozy to keep the machine out of sight and away from little fingers when it is not in use. Always unplug your machine when you are finished sewing.
- Store your fabrics elsewhere: baskets, plastic totes, or vintage suitcases all make wonderful fabric keepers. Use attractive stickers or tags to label your boxes and cases well so you know their contents and can find them easily.
- Keep your minimum sewing essentials—bobbins, scissors, pins, tape measure, and so forth—in a small, easy-to-transport sewing box at your work area. This way you're only moving one box instead of many things you don't need.
- If a standard, folding ironing board is too big for your space, consider using a tabletop or traveling ironing board or a pull-down wall option.
- Be comfortable. Good lighting and proper chairs are essential to a happy sewing environment!

Collaborating with Your Children

Sometimes making things and our creative play happen when we are alone—when children are at school

or napping or late at night after the house is full of sleeping little ones. Sewing is a wonderful way to have some quiet alone time while also creating practical items for your family. I treasure these times, these moments spent alone after a busy day with my children. I have those few moments at the end of the day all to myself, when my thoughts are my own and my creative energy is spent entirely on my own desires. Many of the projects in the book can be made in this kind of environment.

Many of these projects, however, have also been created with the help of—and in some cases, at the insistence of—my children. How incredibly blessed we are to have the most wonderful creative collaborators living right in our own homes! Our family projects are among moments that I will always treasure and

hold close to my heart. In these moments of working together—when their ideas are respected and heard by the adults around them—I see my children shine. Working with them on projects doesn't mean I'm the director and they're the students. It means their ideas need to be respected in the same way that we would respect those of an adult. Some of their ideas might need a little reining in for practical and logistical reasons, but this redirection can always be done gently, with understanding and a bit of guidance to point them in a different direction.

I do believe—if both parent and child desire it—that even the youngest of children can be included in these projects. The extent of their involvement can be as simple as tracing buttons, stacking notions, or playing with bits of fabric. Try asking questions like, "Can you pick out five buttons that you think would look best on this blanket?" or "What kind of artwork do you think would be good on this coat rack for your sister?" The same questions that you would pose to any collaborator—"Do you have any ideas?" "What do you think?"—are warranted when working with little ones.

Encouragement and praise—"Oh, I really, really love that" or "That color looks great there!"—are also essential. Children know you're the parent, so there is no need in creative situations like this to assert any kind of power. Making family projects is about working together and truly respecting each other's ideas and creative work.

Keep in mind, however, that working with children also means that you can't invite a youngster to create with you and then not follow through on his or her ideas. You wouldn't very well invite a friend to work on something with you and then ignore her ideas would you? The same must apply for working with children. Be committed to working with them even if their ideas may pull you away from your original vision for a project. Children are not just the doers; they are also the dreamers—don't deny them that.

As you become accustomed to working with children, you'll find that it is the dreaming that is the most fun and the most inspiring. They will open your eyes to seeing things differently and working in new ways. In turn, you will teach them about working together with other people and provide them with the assistance to realize their dreams and ideas.

Some of the projects in this book involve the use of children's artwork. It is essential that they are involved in these endeavors! Unless they have given it to you, their art belongs to them. Honor that by asking their permission to use it in your projects. Tell them what you'd like to do with it, see if you can involve them in the process of making it, and include them as the creator of the project in name as well. "See what we made!"

Truly the projects that I've made with my children are my favorites of all. They are projects for which I had a small idea that they then expanded upon, or vice versa. Your little ones are people you know so well, and working with that, and with them, can make for a truly beautiful experience—a collaboration of the best kind.

Making Time for the Projects

This effort to make our time at home as rich as possible may initially take some planned dedication. It will mean turning off the television, putting the computer aside for a bit, and setting aside some energy to engage our children at the end of the day when we may feel as though there just isn't any more energy to be found. But what you will quickly realize—or may have already discovered—is that these moments spent with your children to nurture your home life are producers of energy, not just consumers. They will fuel not only your children, but you, too. They will fulfill both your children's need for a sense of home and your own.

Not much about basic sewing techniques has changed in recent decades. Here are some vintage titles, which you might come across in your thrifting journeys, that provide good, basic sewing instruction:

The Vogue Sewing Book
Singer's Sewing Book
The Complete Book of Sewing by Constance Talbot
Better Homes & Gardens Sewing Book

If you'd like more of a contemporary guide, these titles might be of interest to you:

Bend-the-Rules Sewing by Amy Karol
Simplicity's *Simply the Best Sewing Book*
See & Sew: A Sewing Book for Children by Tina Davis

A Guide to the Projects

~~~~~~~~~~~

*T*his guide is intended to be your cheat sheet to the projects found in this book. Here, you'll find all the information, terms, and tools essential to understanding and completing each project. Please read this guide thoroughly before beginning any of the projects, so you'll have everything you need to know to make your project fun and successful!

At the beginning of each project, you'll find some details to give you a full picture of what to expect. Those details are defined as follows:

Difficulty Levels

Beginner: Assumes little previous sewing knowledge. Most beginner projects are suitable for older children (at least 10 years of age).

Intermediate: Assumes some previous sewing knowledge.

Advanced: Assumes previous sewing knowledge as well as familiarity with binding and buttonholes.

Length of Time

Each project is given a rough estimate of length of time to completion, fitting into these categories: half day, full day, weekend, and season. These are maximum, very generous timeframes, as they allow for lots of living to happen around the making—including children and stopping for breaks. The time it takes you to complete a project will vary greatly depending on how you adapt the pattern, how much sewing you've done in the past, and how involved little ones are, but I hope the time estimates will give you some sense of how long a particular project can take.

Suitable for Little Hands

You'll find this note on some of the projects in each section of the book, and each of those projects contains something specific for children to do in the process. Of course, many more projects in this book may be suitable for children depending on their skills and your comfort levels. Read through the pattern, or try making one yourself, to determine other ways to include your children and their interests in a project. See "Collaborating with Your Children" on page 14 for more ideas on making sewing a successful and positive experience for both you and your child.

Use What You Have

This book isn't about making things exactly as I make them. While you'll certainly find the patterns with specific instructions to get you started in the right direction, nothing you make will be exactly the same as the sample project—or exactly like anyone else would make it either. By the very nature of repurposed and vintage materials, we are giving our creative efforts their very own, one-of-a-kind, unique look. What you make will

truly be your own creation. Your own imagination and your own hands will work together to create something beautiful. This is the true beauty of handmade. I wish you much fun and creative joy as you breathe life into these projects and share them with your family!

Tools You Need

I've included many details in the Materials section of each project so you'll know specifically what you need as you go along. However, each project assumes you have the following essentials:

- A sewing machine and all the essential tools needed for maintaining and running it (See Finding Vintage and Thrifted Materials on page 10 for tips on purchasing your own.)
- Scissors, for cutting only fabric and kept separate from your other household scissors so they stay sharp
- Regular scissors, for cutting pattern pieces and nonfabric items
- Needles, for hand-sewing
- Pincushion
- Ironing board and iron
- Pins
- Pencil
- Safety pins, in a variety of sizes
- Tape measure, flexible cloth or plastic, not metal or wood
- Yardstick
- Sewing thread (I prefer 100-percent cotton, but using thrifted polyester thread is an option as well.)
- Sewing machine needles (I used size 11 throughout the projects unless mentioned otherwise.)
- Seam ripper

Optional, but quite nice to have on hand:

- Tailor's chalk
- Fabric pens and markers
- Small scissors, small embroidery scissors, or thread snippers, for trim work
- Pinking shears
- Tracing paper
- Rotary blade
- Thimble
- Bias tape maker, in a variety of sizes
- Cutting mat

Glossary of Terms Used in the Projects

The following terms are referred to often in the projects:

Backstitch. To stitch forward and backward several times at the beginning of a seam for a few stitches. Backstitching helps to prevent seams from unraveling and holds the ends securely in place.

Baste stitch. A stitch meant to temporarily hold sewing in place. This is achieved by increasing the stitch length on your machine. If basting stitches are visible in the finished project, they can easily be pulled out either by hand or with a seam ripper. Backstitching is unnecessary when baste stitching.

Blind stitch. A hand stitch that leaves only a tiny bit of the stitch showing on the top. Stitches should be no more than 1/8" apart.

Box pleat. A double pleat created by folding fabric under on either side of it.

Edgestitch. To stitch close to the edge of a hem or fold.

Running stitch: A small, even stitch made with embroidery floss. The space between the stitches should be equal to the length of the stitches.

Slip stitch: A stitch used to pull two folded edges together, such as the binding on a quilt. Make a slip stitch by running a needle and thread through the inside of one fold, and then coming out to pick up a few threads on the other side.

Topstitch: To sew a row of stitches close to the outside finished edge of a garment or object, for either a decorative effect or for an increase in the security of your seams.

Seam Allowance

All patterns call for a 1/2" seam unless otherwise noted. The projects also assume you will backstitch at the beginning and end of each seam and that you will remove pins as you go.

Using the Patterns in this Book

You'll find all the pattern templates in the back of the book. If instructed, enlarge as necessary at your local copy center. Use tracing paper to trace and create your own pattern pieces.

Part Two

THE PROJECTS

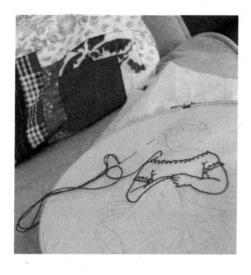

1

Nourish

Projects to inspire Family Feasts

~~~~~~~~~~~~~~~~~~~~~~

The patterns and projects in Nourish are all about celebrating the ways in which we nourish ourselves, our children, and our homes. They explore the ways in which we "feed" our families—both literally and figuratively. Here, I hope you will find ideas on nourishing your family's mind, body, and spirit—enough to inspire many a family feast!

Broadturn Bag

~~~~~~~~~~

A s the season of a CSA (community supported agriculture) farm grows, so does the produce coming home! When summer peaked at our CSA, Broadturn Farm (featured on page 46 in "At the Farm"), my children and I found ourselves needing just a few more bags to carry home all the bounty and beauty of our farm share. I really wanted to make something I could sling over my shoulder easily. The bag design had to make hauling produce less of a chore yet still give me the ability to carry a babe on my hip or to bend down and greet the bunnies on our way out of the farmyard. After a morning spent sewing with a favorite, but worn and stained, tablecloth, I had enough bags to carry with us to the farm—and more than enough to replace all of our other grocery bags as well. The size of this bag also makes it a suitable size for all the little helpers you may have on market day, particularly if they wear it messenger style, as Ezra is in the photograph.

Pattern Details

Intermediate
A half-day project
Finished size: 14″ × 13″

Use What You Have

Old tablecloths provide an excellent fabric weight for this bag. The crisp cotton used in most old tablecloths is strong enough to hold a bag full of groceries while still having a bit of stretch, making it suitable for carrying objects of varying shapes and sizes. But any heavyweight cotton will work beautifully for this project. (*The photographed bag is made from a thrifted vintage tablecloth.*)

Materials

Approximately 1 yard total, as follows:

Fabric 1: (2) 15″ × 5″ pieces for the bottom
Fabric 2: (2) 15″ × 15″ pieces for the bag panels
Fabric 3: (1) 34″ × 8″ piece for the strap
Pattern piece A (found on page 180)

1. PREPARE MATERIALS

Gather all materials and cut all fabrics to the measurements given above.

2. PREPARE PATTERN PIECES

Cut out pattern piece A, and use it to cut out two bag bottoms from the 15″ × 5″ pieces of fabric.

3. SEW THE FRONT AND BACK PIECES

Place the two 15″ × 15″ main panel pieces right sides together. Pin the pieces together on two opposite sides. To create the side seams, stitch down these two sides. Press the seams open.

4. SEW BOTTOM PIECES

Place both bottom pieces wrong sides together and pin. Stitch around entire bottom (through both layers), 1/8″ from the edge.

5. ASSEMBLE BAG

Lay the sewn bottom piece on a flat surface. Attach the sewn main bag panel to the bottom, right sides together, by pinning the side seams to the dots corresponding to the places on the pattern piece.

Stitch in place around the entire bottom of bag. Repeat the stitching 1/8″ away (toward the inside) from the first line of stitching.

Using pinking shears to avoid fraying, trim the seam by cutting the seam allowance close to the stitching, but without touching the stitches. Cut slits along the edge of the curved corners. Be careful not to get too close to the stitching.

Turn the bag right side out.

EARTHY TIP

As a society, our consumption of plastic bags averages about one million per minute these days, with an average life of nearly 1,000 years each. While awareness of their harmful effects and the increase in reusable bags grow, many gaps in our usage are painfully obvious. We may bring our own bags to the grocery store, but do we bring them on our other shopping trips, such as to the pharmacy, the thrift shop, or the department store? Make plenty of these Broadturn Bags so you'll have extras to bring along with you wherever you shop!

6. HEM BAG TOP

At the top of the bag, fold the top edge ¼″ toward the inside of the bag. Press. Fold again ½″ toward the inside of the bag. Press. Edgestitch.

7. MAKE STRAP

To make the strap, first fold the 34″ × 8″ strap fabric in half lengthwise. Press to create a crease, and open. Fold lengthwise again, bringing the two outer edges in to the center crease. Press. Do not open. Fold lengthwise again on the original center crease, making a strap that is 2″ wide by 34″ long. Stitch down both long sides of the strap, ⅛″ in from the edge.

8. FINISH BAG

Fold short ends of strap in ¼″ to encase the raw edge. Place one end of the strap evenly across the inside seam of the bag, making sure the raw edge is sandwiched between the bag and the strap. The bottom edge of the strap should be 1″ below the bag's top. Pin. Repeat with other strap, checking that the strap is not twisted. Pin. Stitch the strap ends in place, sewing a square to secure the strap 1″ below the bag's top hem and even with the bag's top hem.

Millie's Hot Pad

~~~~~~~~~

I found this old, much-used, and worn hot pad (or trivet, pot holder, or oven mitt, depending on your preference) among my grandmother's things many years ago. Despite its worn seam and faded fabrics, something about its quilting and petite nature appealed to me. Once I brought it home, it rather quickly became my favorite hot pad—the one I always reached for above all the others. It was clear that the remainder of its life was to be a short one with me and all the energetic little helpers I have in my kitchen. And so I set to work on recreating it, just as how I imagined my grandmother—or great grandmother, perhaps—had made hers one day many years ago.

Pattern Details

Intermediate
A half-day project
Finished size: 6½″

Use What You Have

This project is excellent for using up your scraps and smaller pieces of fabric. The hot pads are a great use for smaller vintage pieces that you want to really show off without using too much of the fabric. Feedsacks are the perfect material for both the history and the function related to this project. The center batting of the hot pad can be made from thick, old towels or from newly purchased cotton batting. (*The photographed hot pad is made from vintage feedsack scraps with a thrifted towel as the batting.*)

Materials

Approximately ½ yard total, as follows:

Fabric: (4) 7″ × 7″ pieces for the hot pad
Batting: (2) 7″ × 7″ thrifted old towels or new cotton batting
Extra-wide, double-fold bias tape: 20″ long
Pattern pieces B, C, and D (found on pages 181–83)

1. PREPARE MATERIALS

Gather all materials and cut all fabrics to the measurements given above.

2. PREPARE PATTERN PIECES

Cut pattern pieces B, C, and D. Using pattern B, cut one piece from the fabric for the front middle. Using pattern C, cut two pieces from the fabric for the front sides. Using pattern D, cut one piece from the fabric for the back and cut two pieces from the batting.

CRAFTY TIP

"Feedsack" is a term for vintage fabrics that were used as sacks to hold sugar and flour in the nineteenth and early twentieth century. Once the contents of the sacks were used or emptied, women repurposed the sacks' fabric into all manner of things for the household. When manufacturers realized the trend, they began printing more colorful fabrics and adding patterns on the insides of the sacks. Feedsacks stopped being produced in the 1960s, but the fabric pieces still remain and are a bit of historic treasure for many crafters today.

3. PIECE BATTING AND FRONT HOT PAD

Begin by placing the two layers of batting one on top of the other. On top of them, place the front middle piece (B) in the center, right side up.

Press the straight edge of both side pieces (C) under ¼". Place one side piece on each side of the center piece (B), right sides up. Align the outer edge with the circle of the batting on both sides. The straight edges of the side pieces will overlap the center piece slightly. Pin the pieces in place. Edgestitch close to the pressed edges on the straight sides of both side pieces, through all layers. This step forms the hot pad top.

4. SEW HOT PAD

Now lay the back piece (D) on a surface, wrong side up. On top of this, place the hot pad top evenly, with batting side down. Baste around the circle close to the edge, sewing all of the layers together as one. Trim the edges of the entire circle, being careful not to get too close to your stitching.

5. ATTACH BIAS BINDING

Lay the hot pad on a flat surface, front side up. Open the bias tape fully. Lay the open bias tape on top of the front side of the hot pad, matching the raw edge of the bias tape with the raw edge of the circle. Stitch the tape in place, sewing ¼″ in from the edge. Continue around the entire circle, turning the binding as needed in order to follow the curve of the hot pad's edge. When you get to the starting point, continue to place the binding around the edge, overlapping the existing binding by ½″ to complete the circle and encase the binding. Cut the remaining bias tape.

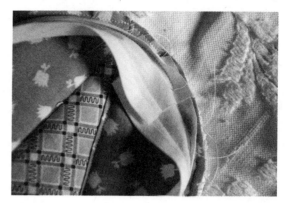

6. FINISH HOT PAD

Fold the bias binding and its folded edge over the edge of the pot holder to the back side of the potholder. Press if necessary to smooth out the hot pad. Pin the binding in place. Attach the binding by hand-sewing it to the back layer. Sew completely around the circle. A slip stitch or blind stitch works well here.

Family Art Table Runner

This project is a marriage of my two favorite things: children's art and our family meals! As far as I can tell, no refrigerator ever has enough spots for children's art, and none of us ever has enough opportunities to sit and talk about our children's art. This table runner gives us the opportunity to display our children's art as well as give us a chance to gush over it—and all during the celebration and feasting of a family meal. The only way to make the occasion better is to add a little dessert for a perfect family gathering!

Pattern Details

Intermediate
Weekend project
Finished size: 49″ × 13″

Use What You Have

The base of this table runner can be constructed from a variety of different fabrics; however, the heavier the fabric, the better the runner will stay in place on the table. A bed coverlet, painter's canvas, burlap sack, or even wool blankets are all appropriate for this project. (*The photographed runner is made from linen, with fabric scraps for the patchwork strips.*)

Materials

Approximately 1½ yards total, plus scraps for the patchwork:

Fabric 1: (1) 50″ × 14″ piece for the top
Fabric 2: (1) 50″ × 14″ piece for the bottom
Fabric 3: (6) 5″ × 5″ pieces for the patchwork
Rick rack: 3 yards, plus more if additional artwork is used
Up to (3) 8½″ × 11″ printable fabric sheets (available at your local craft store)
Your child's artwork (on a white background)
Access to a scanner and printer

I. PREPARE MATERIALS

Gather all materials and cut all fabrics to the measurements given above.

2. PREPARE YOUR CHILD'S ARTWORK

Scan your child's artwork, size it to fit the fabric sheet, and then print it on the fabric sheet following the manufacturer's instructions. This project can accommodate up to three full-sized fabric sheets. The photographed project features just one sheet in the center. (If you do not have access to a scanner at home or work, take your children's artwork to a local office supply store and either ask one of the associates to scan and print the artwork on fabric paper for you, or do it yourself using the store's self-serve machines.)

3. PIECE PATCHWORK

Begin piecing together the two patchwork strips. Use three squares for each. With the right sides together, stitch one square to another with a seam allowance of $1/4''$. Press the seams open. Turn each long $14''$-side of both strips under $1/4''$ toward the wrong side. Press. Set the patchwork strips aside.

4. PREPARE TOP OF TABLE RUNNER

Lay the top fabric piece flat, right side up. Place the artwork on the fabric as desired. Pin in place. Place the two fabric strips on the top fabric piece, $4''$ in from each short side of the runner top. Pin in place. Stitch these pieces (artwork and patchwork strips) to the top fabric piece by sewing $1/8''$ in from the edges of the pieces.

Align the rick rack along each long edge of the patchwork strips, covering the stitching and the fold. Pin the rick rack in place, and trim it as needed (you'll use two $14''$ lengths of rick rack per patchwork strip). Using thread the same color as the rick rack, machine stitch the rick rack down its center.

Use one long piece of rick rack for the artwork. Start in one corner. When you reach the next corner, fold the rick rack over, creating a 90-degree angle. Pin it in place as you go. When you return to your starting point, overlap the rick rack by 1/4". Attach the rick rack to the artwork by machine stitching it in place.

5. ATTACH BOTTOM FABRIC

Lay the bottom piece, right side up, on a flat surface. Place your finished top piece, right side down, on top of the bottom piece. (The right sides will be together.) Pin the pieces in place. Beginning in the center of one short side, stitch around all four sides of the runner, stopping 4" before your starting point. Trim the corners.

6. FINISH TABLE RUNNER

Turn the runner right side out through the opening, gently pushing out the four corners with a chopstick or pencil eraser, if necessary, to create defined points. Press. Topstitch around all four sides of the runner, 1/2" in from the edge. This final step will close the opening on the short side.

Maddie's Rag Rug

~~~~~~~~~~

*T*hough the popularity of making rag rugs has ebbed and flowed through the centuries, the tradition has stayed alive. Rooted deep in handcrafting for family life, rag rugs carry the essence and the history of repurposing as a necessity as well as an art. Rag rugs can be made in a number of different ways, and you will find many sources to learn about them (see the resources at the back of the book). If you're lucky, you might have the greatest learning source of all in a living relative who can teach you the skill. My Great Aunt Maddie was a rag rug maker, and with her passing, my family was left with a plethora of rag rugs that she made over the past century. All of them were created from clothing and other household items that she also made.

When I added one of Aunt Maddie's rugs to my home, I was inspired to create the same myself and carefully studied her rugs to discern the method she used. Making rag rugs has turned into a wonderful way for me to extend the life of some fabrics and clothing my family loves, keep our home cozy and warm, and connect to our past.

Pattern Details

Intermediate
A season
Finished size: As desired

Use What You Have

Many different fabrics work well for rag rugs; however, to have a uniform thickness, it's helpful to use similarly weighted fabrics. Standard-weight cotton clothing works fine, as well as heavier wool, denim, corduroy, and chamois. (*The photographed rug is made from midweight cotton clothing—shirts, pants, rags, and dishtowels.*)

Materials

Fabric: Discarded clothing of the same fabric weight
Lacing cord
Hand-quilting thread
Heavy-duty needle (with a blunt tip and a large eye)
Darning needle

I. PREPARE MATERIALS

Gather all materials as described above. (The gathering process of this project may take several weeks or months, depending upon the availability of fabric.) As you collect fabrics, you may want to sort them by color, shade, or pattern, cut and sew them into strips, then roll them into a ball as explained below to keep your piles neat. I usually just cut it as I go, without worrying about color order, making the rug a bit more of a surprise in color at the end.

To prepare your materials, cut the fabric into 2″ strips of any length. Cut the short ends. To join the strips, place the two strips of fabric, right sides together, and then stitch a ⅝″ seam. Roll the fabric strips into a ball, as you would yarn.

Continue cutting strips and sewing them together until you have a large ball about 6″ or more in diameter. Make three balls.

2. BRAID STRIPS

When you have three large balls, you can prepare the strips for braiding. Begin by folding the two raw edges of your strips in toward the wrong side of the fabric, approximately ¼″ on each side. Press. Continue along the entire length of ball, rewinding it as you go. Repeat this process for the other two balls.

Take one end from each of your three fabric balls and loop the three strips together, forming a loose knot. Place the knot on a doorknob or a hook to begin braiding.

3. COIL AND LACE BRAID

Using a classic three-strand braid, braid until the strand is approximately 10″ long, at which point you can start to coil the braid.

First remove the braid from the doorknob, tighten the knot, and cut off any excess strands before the knot.

Next create a tight spiral with the braid. Hold the braid in place by lacing the braids rather than stitching them. Using a lacing cord and a heavy-duty needle, weave the needle and cord from one strand of the braid on one side to another strand of the braid on the opposite side of the coil to which it is connected.

Work a few feet in braiding and then do a bit of lacing. You'll be working on your lap at the beginning and moving the coiled braid to the floor as the rug grows. Keep braiding and lacing until you are satisfied with the size of the rug Braided rugs can be any size—for everything from a dollhouse-sized rug to a mat for a table to a full-sized rug. The size of your rug depends on your patience, interest, and amount of materials at hand.

4. FINISH RAG RUG

To finish, trim the three strands to the same length and fold them over approximately 1/2", covering the raw edge. Lay this piece flat against the rug, and complete the lacing. Secure the ends to the rug with regular heavy-weight thread and a darning needle.

calvin's papier-mâché bowls

~~~~~~~~~~

*P*apier-mâché is one of the most frequently requested craft projects by my little ones. Calvin most of all loves to make these bowls for storing all the special treasures that his seven-year-old self collects—rocks, pinecones, corks, bottle caps, and marbles. He makes a bowl for each collection. By using an existing bowl as a mold, this project is satisfying and successful for even the youngest among us. Don't let papier-mâché intimidate you—it's really just a matter of "making a big pile of glue and newspaper and turning it into something!" as Calvin tells me. He's right. Though, if you'd like more specific instructions, read on.

Pattern Details

Beginner
A half-day project (plus drying time)
Suitable for little hands
Finished size: As desired

Use What You Have

This wonderful project is perfect for repurposing some of those piles of paper that I'm sure are around your home—mail, envelopes, newspaper, copy paper, and more. Thin paper works best. Heavier paper, such as grocery bags, is a bit more difficult to manipulate. Lightweight paper alone is a little too thin, however, it can make for a nice layer on top of other papers. (*The photographed bowls, 8" in diameter, are made from newspaper and a final layer of decorative tissue paper.*)

Materials

Paper: Thin papers, such as newspaper, cut into 1" × 5" strips
Bowl to use as a mold
Tinfoil or plastic wrap
Paste (see recipe in the Crafty Tip on page 45, or purchase premade paste at art supply stores)
Paintbrush for applying paste
Optional: gesso for smoothing out layers at the end (similar to a primer, available at art supply stores)
Optional: Acrylic paint for finishing

I. PREPARE MATERIALS

Gather all materials and cut the paper to the measurements given above. Prepare a surface on which to work, as the paste can be messy. I keep old vinyl tablecloths around for these kinds of projects. A layer of newspaper also works well.

Prepare your bowl as a mold by placing it upside down on the work surface and covering it tightly with foil or plastic wrap. Smooth out the foil or wrap.

2. PASTE STRIPS TO MOLD

Use a paintbrush to apply a layer of paste to one side of a newspaper strip, and then apply the strip to the covered bowl. Repeat until the entire bowl has been encased in at least four layers. There is no need to wait for each layer to dry before starting another layer.

For a sturdier bowl, finish with a layer of computer paper atop the newspaper layers. Use the paintbrush and your fingers to smooth out all the wrinkles at the final layer.

Let the bowl dry. Depending on the humidity, this process can take several days. In the sun, it might take just one day.

3. REMOVE PAPER BOWL FROM MOLD

When the bowl is completely dry, remove your new bowl from its mold by carefully and slowly lifting the foil or wrap from the original bowl mold. Then gently remove the foil or wrap from the papier-mâché.

4. FINISH BOWL

I like to use a thin layer of gesso to further smooth out the bowl and provide a good base to apply paint. With acrylic paints, you can paint the outside and inside of your bowls. (*Note:* Papier-mâché bowls are not suitable for food).

CRAFTY TIP

Making your own papier-mâché paste is economical, easy, and fun. Simply combine ½ cup of flour, 2½ cups of water, and 1 tablespoon of salt in a saucepan. Cook the mixture on medium heat, stirring often, until it forms a gluelike paste (about five to ten minutes). Add one drop of clove oil to prevent the glue from turning moldy. Let the mixture cool. Stir before using. Unused paste can be stored in a glass jar to be used within seven days.

At the Farm

Nobody made a greater mistake than he who did
nothing because he could only do a little.

—EDMUND BURKE

Much of the way my children measure and talk about the passing of time is by the changing of the seasons; it seems so much more tangible to them than the calendar months and years to which we adults adhere. Children are fully aware of how humid it may feel, how blue the blueberries may be, or how much cooler the evenings have become. The names of the months? That concept doesn't mean a lot to them at these young ages. That the mosquitoes are beginning to appear, that the snow is melting . . . These things they can understand. It's a different measure of time, one more inherent in their senses and in their bodies—right where children "are." It's a connection to the earth that many of us had as children, too, but somewhere along the way, it has disappeared or, at the least, quieted.

One of the most wonderful gifts our family received has been the joy of connecting to a local, organic, community-supported farm and the farmers who tend it. John Bliss and Stacy Brenner, along with their two children, Emma and Flora, are the farmers at Broadturn Farm. With complete adoration, our children call them Farmer John and Farmer Stacy. Repurposed in the truest sense of the word, the farm—all 400 acres of it—was dormant for years until it was resurrected by the area land trust. John and Stacy breathed their fresh vision into the farm, bringing it back to life in a way much like its original purpose, but they adapted to modern needs and wants. The farm now runs as a successful CSA (community supported agriculture), providing organic, local, and fresh food to area families project (see the Broadturn Bag on page 27 for a project inspired by this wonderful program). But more than that, the farm offers the opportunity for a real connection to the food we eat and to the earth on which it was grown and raised.

And so, each and every week during the harvest season, and often during off season, in a comfortable and dependable rhythm, we make our small trek to the farm for nourishment of our bodies, our minds, and our spirits. The children gather our Broadturn Bags in preparation, and we walk to the farm, stopping along the way to say hello to the cow, the pigs, the ducks, the chicks, the bunnies, and whatever butterflies may be in the flower garden. And then we journey on to gather our produce for the week. We've established a solid routine: Adelaide does the measuring, Calvin loves counting the food, and Ezra's job is gathering just the right eggs by his standards. All are very important details in our journey to collect our food.

Very few outings are easy for me with three young children and just one adult. The beach, the woods, and the farm—those are easy, fun, and wonderful. The hardest part is the leaving, which no one ever wants to do. But, thankfully, the leaving is always softened by the anticipation of getting our food home and on the table.

Supporting your local farm is an excellent and most delicious way to help sustain your local food community. To find a CSA farm in your area, visit www.localharvest.org. There, you'll also find information on your local farmers' market, food co-op, and natural grocery stores.

2

Nurture

Projects to inspire
wellness and care

~~~~~~

The patterns and projects in Nurture are intended to inspire wellness and care in your family. These projects will
add a little bit of comfort, love, and heart to the ways
in which you care for each other in times of sickness, in
times of health, and in times of need—the everyday little
moments that matter so very much.

Rag Bag

~~~~~~~~

*T*he family rag bag, the place where stained clothing, old towels, and stray socks spend the remainder of their lives as rags for cleaning, is not so common these days. Over the years, many of us may have strayed to the convenience of paper towels, but switching back to cloth provides many advantages. In addition to the lack of paper consumed, cleaning with cloth also extends the life of fabrics and fibers. But best of all, cloth—especially 100-percent cotton—is a better cleaning material because of its absorbency and versatility. The more densely woven the fabric is, the more effective it will be for cleaning.

This handy bag makes an eye-pleasing and convenient home for your rags as you wait for cleaning time.

Pattern Details

Intermediate (requires application of a
   buttonhole)
A half-day project
Finished size: 11″ × 11″

Use What You Have

The fabric needed for this project is quite versatile. Cotton tablecloths work wonderfully because of their sturdy, thick cotton, but any cotton, canvas, or linen fabric will work equally well. Use any kind of fabric scraps for the fabric balls. (*The photographed rag bag is made from a vintage cotton tablecloth with cotton fabric scraps for the balls and bias binding for the straps and ties.*)

Materials

Approximately 1 yard total, as follows:

Fabric 1: (1) 12″ × 28″ for the bag
Fabric 2: (6) 4″ × 10″ scraps for the balls
Embroidery floss: (6) 30″ long
Embroidery floss: (6) 6″ long
Embroidery needle
Double-fold extra-wide bias tape for straps: (2)
   18″ long
Double-fold extra-wide bias tape for drawstring: (1) 30″ long
Buttonhole foot for sewing machine
Pinking shears

1. PREPARE MATERIALS

Gather all materials and cut all fabrics to the measurements given above.

2. MAKE FABRIC BALLS

Begin by making the fabric balls. Taking one piece at a time, wrap the raw edge under itself and begin to roll the fabric. Tuck in the ends as you go along, forming the fabric into a rounded and tight ball shape.

Using the 30″ length of embroidery floss in a color of your choosing, wrap the fabric ball tightly to keep its round shape. Wind until you have a 4″ length of the embroidery floss left, and then tie a knot to the other end of the strand. Cut away the excess floss. Repeat this step for all six fabric balls, and set them aside.

3. PREPARE BAG

Fold the bag fabric piece in half lengthwise, with right sides together, so that it measures 12″ × 14″. With the fold at the bottom, sew a seam down both 14″ sides. Trim both seams close to the stitching without cutting into the stitches.

Turn the bag right side out. Along the bottom fold, measure and mark six evenly spaced points with a pencil. The marks will be approximately 1 ½″ apart.

4. ATTACH FABRIC BALLS

Thread a needle with 6″ of embroidery floss. Coming from the inside of the bag, pull the needle out just slightly to one side of one pencil mark along the bottom seam, leaving at least a 2″ tail inside the bag. With the needle, pick up a few strands of the embroidery floss and a bit of fabric on one of the fabric balls. Place the needle just to the other side of the marked pencil spot on the bag, and pull the needle to the inside of the bag. Remove the needle from the floss. From the inside, pull both ends of the strand tightly to bring the ball to the edge of the fabric fold. Tie the ends securely with a double overhand knot. Cut the excess floss. Repeat this step for all six fabric balls.

5. HEM BAG TOP

At the top of the bag, which is still right side out, fold the raw edge toward the inside ¼″. Press. Edgestitch.

6. MAKE THE BUTTONHOLES

Choose one side of the bag to be the front. Place the buttonholes by measuring approximately 5½″ in from each side and 3″ down from the top; mark this spot lightly with a dot in pencil or tailor's chalk. Using this dot as the top point for the two vertical buttonholes, measure ½″ lower than the dots and mark a straight line, ½″ long, moving from the top measurement toward the bottom of the bag. This line is your buttonhole guide.

Create two buttonholes using your machine's buttonhole foot and instructions. Cut each buttonhole open with sharp scissors or a razor.

7. MAKE DRAWSTRING CASING

Fold 2″ of the top edge toward the inside of bag. Press. Edgestitch. This will cover the back of your buttonholes, creating a casing. Complete the casing for the drawstring by stitching around the entire top of the bag, 1″ down from the top folded edge. This line of stitching should be at the top of the buttonholes.

8. MAKE STRAPS

Make the straps by stitching an 18″ length of bias tape close to the edge to close the binding. (To prevent the bias binding from slipping into the plate of your sewing machine as you begin to sew, hold the thread from your bobbin and spoon taut as you begin stitching. Use these threads to guide and gently pull the binding until the seam gets started.) Trim each end with pinking shears. Repeat this process for the second strap.

Along the casing stitching on the inside of the bag, measure out 2½″ from both sides of each vertical seam. Pin both ends of one strap to the front of the bag; pin both ends of the other strap to the back of the bag. The ends of the strap should just touch the casing stitching. Stitch the straps in place with a zigzag stitch.

9. FINISH RAG BAG

Make the drawstring by stitching the 30″ length of bias tape close the edge to close the binding. Trim each end with pinking shears.

Secure one end of the drawstring to a large safety pin and place it inside one of the buttonholes. Using the safety pin to guide the drawstring through the casing, work the drawstring around the bag and out through the second buttonhole. Work slowly and carefully when you get to each side seam to get the drawstring past the seam fabric. Adjust and center the drawstring, tying it in a decorative bow. Remove the safety pin.

TOWEL RUG

~~~~~~~~~~~

*W*ith busy little ones in and out of the bathroom—and the spills and the messes and the mud that follow them—nothing beats a bathroom rug that can be tossed right in the washing machine and hung out on the line to dry quickly. This project, which also provides the comfortable feeling of *standing on a worn in, soft towel*, can be easily adapted to your own design and taste. It's also a wonderful project for showcasing some of those funky retro towels from your youth! Use this pattern as a base for what works well in your home and with your style.

Pattern Details

Intermediate
A half-day project
Finished size: 34″ × 21″

Use What You Have

This project will make excellent use of bath towels and cotton sheets no longer in use or purchased used. (*The photographed rug is made from a vintage sheet for the base and vintage towels for the back and the strips.*)

Materials

Approximately 2 yards total, as follows:

Fabric 1: (1) 34″ × 21″ piece of cotton for the top
Fabric 2: (1) 34″ × 21″ bath towel for the rug bottom (*Note:* If you do not have a towel this large, piece together strips of towel to get the proper size.)
Fabric 3: (8) 2″ × 22″ strips of towel for the top
Optional: Puffy fabric paint (available from local arts and craft supply store)

1. PREPARE MATERIALS

Gather all materials and cut all fabrics to the measurements given above.

2. PIECE RUG TOP

Lay the 34" × 21" piece of cotton fabric flat, right side up. Arrange the eight towel strips as desired on top of the cotton fabric, and pin them in place. Stitch the towel strips to the cotton fabric ⅛" away from the raw edges.

3. PREPARE RUG BOTTOM

Place the large towel (the bottom of the rug) right side up. On top of the towel, place the rug top you just completed, right side down. Pin together. Beginning on one of the long sides, stitch around all four sides, stopping 4" before you come to your starting point.

Trim the corners. Turn the rug right side out, gently pushing out the four corners with a pencil or chopstick, if necessary.

4. FINISH TOWEL RUG

Press the rug flat. Topstitch around all four sides of the bath math, approximately ¼″ from the edge. Close the 4″ opening as you go.

Depending on your bathroom floor and the towel you used for the bottom, the mat could be slippery. If this is the case, apply strips of puffy fabric paint to the bottom of mat.

Cut the appliqué along the traced lines. Place it on the right side of one flannel piece as desired. Pin the appliqué in place. Machine stitch close to the appliqué's edge to attach it to the flannel.

4. ATTACH FRONT AND BACK FABRICS

Place the front and back fabric pieces right sides together. Pin them in place. Stitch around three sides of the fabric, leaving the top open. Trim the seams, clip the curves, and turn the flannel right side out through the top opening.

Unbutton the cover at this point to open the cozy. Turn the top raw edge toward the wrong side of fabric 1/2". Press. Repeat, folding the edge another 1/2", and press. Remove any buttons that will be in the way of stitching this top fold. Edgestitch.

5. FINISH HEALING COZY

Slip a filled hot water bottle in the cover and button the cozy. When you need to empty or refill the water bottle, remove it from the cover.

silky eye pillow

~~~~~~~~~~

*S*ometimes the best kind of healing we can give or receive is the emotional kind. The ability to relax, meditate, and take a break from it all are essential to children. These eye pillows are favorites around here because of the soothing way in which they help our young ones slow down, breathe, and rest their minds for a moment. We put on some favorite mellow music, or tell a story, and let them drift into a place of peace. And when Mama or Papa is in need of some relaxation, we make sure there's a Silky Eye Pillow nearby for the grown-ups in the family, too.

Pattern Details

Beginner
A half-day project
Finished size: 8½" × 4½"

Use What You Have

This pattern calls for a 100-percent silk scarf for the outer pillow cover fabric. The pillow insert calls for a lightweight cotton. Muslin is ideal, but any cotton will work. (*The photographed eye pillow is made from a vintage scarf, and the insert is made from lightweight cotton quilting muslin.*)

Materials

Approximately ½ yard fabric total, as follows:

Fabric 1: (2) 9" × 5" cotton pieces for pillow insert
Fabric 2: (2) 5½" × 7" silk pieces for pillow cover
Fabric 3: (1) 9½" × 5½" silk piece for pillow cover
Filling 1: 1½ cups total of one or more ingredients: flaxseed, buckwheat hulls, and/or rice
Filling 2: 1 teaspoon dried chamomile
Filling 3: 1 teaspoon dried lavender
(*Note:* All fillings are available at a natural foods store.)
Serving spoon

I. PREPARE MATERIALS

Gather all materials and cut all fabrics to the measurements given above.

2. MAKE PILLOW INSERT

Place the two pillow insert fabric pieces right sides together. Pin them in place. Beginning in the middle of one long side, stitch around all four sides, stopping 2″ before your starting point on the long side. Trim the corners, being careful to avoid cutting the stitches.

Turn the sewn pieces right side out through the 2″ opening. Use your fingers or a chopstick to gently push out the four corners.

3. PREPARE FILLINGS

In a bowl, mix the flaxseed, dried chamomile, and lavender. Using a spoon, fill the pillow insert through the opening on the side.

Sliding the seeds and herbs to the opposite side, sew a zigzag stitch down the entire length of one long side where the opening was. Set the insert aside.

CRAFTY TIP

When sewing with a lightweight fabric such as silk, you'll want to adjust your sewing machine needle size for better sewing results. A size 9 needle is generally best for silk fabrics.

4. MAKE PILLOW COVER

Lay one of the 5 1/2″ × 7″ pieces right side down on a flat surface. On one of the short sides, fold the edge over 1/4″ toward the wrong side. Press using a low or silk setting on an iron. Repeat, folding the edge over 1/2″. Press again. Edgestitch. Repeat the process for the second piece.

Place the 9 1/2″ × 5 1/2″ pillow cover piece right side up on a flat surface. On top of this piece, place one of the smaller pillow cover pieces right side down, aligning one short edge with a short edge on the larger piece. Lay the other smaller pillow cover piece right side down, aligning one short edge with the short edge on the opposite side of the larger piece. Pin all three pieces in place.

Stitch around all four sides of the fabric pillow, backstitching over the side spots where the three layers overlap. Trim the corners, being careful to avoid cutting the stitches.

5. FINISH EYE PILLOW

Turn the pillow right side out at the overlapping point in the middle. Use a chopstick or a pencil to gently push out the four corners, if necessary. Press. Insert the pillow insert through the same overlapping opening. Remove the insert from the pillow cover to hand-wash the cover as needed.

cloth Diapers

~~~~~~~~

*E*arly in my first pregnancy, my husband and I decided that cloth diapers would be the best choice for our family. A huge factor in our decision was environmental impact. (It can take up to 500 years for a disposable diaper to biodegrade, not to mention the toxic effects of producing said diaper.) But in addition to the effect on the earth, we considered the effects of the same toxins—from bleach to dioxin—on our baby's skin. We chose a cloth alternative not only for its gentleness on the earth, but also for its gentleness on our child's skin. Fortunately many alternatives are now available for more natural and less toxic diapering alternatives.

Should cloth diapers be the right choice for your family, I encourage you to give these simple-to-make and easy-to-care-for cloth diapers a go. I found it so rewarding to breathe new life into something that we had once used and worn, in the very same way that many generations of mothers before me had done.

Pattern Details

Intermediate
A day project (to create a plentiful stash)
Finished sizes: 12″ × 13″ (17″ × 20″) fits infant
(toddler)

Use What You Have

Old T-shirts, flannel sheets and shirts, and preloved jersey baby blankets all make excellent diaper material. Don't hesitate to stray outside of the white/neutral color zone, either. Diapers can truly be a rainbow of colors! If you are looking to purchase new fabric for your cloth diapers, consider buying organic cotton or hemp as a more agriculturally sus-tainable option. Find more at www.organiccotton plus.com. (*The photographed diapers are made from a combination of old T-shirts for the inside layers and a set of flannel bedsheets for the outer layer.*)

Materials

Approximately 1 yard total per diaper, as follows:

Fabric 1: (4) 12″ × 13″ (17″ × 20″) pieces for the diaper fabric
Fabric 2: (2) 4″ × 13″ (6″ × 20″) pieces for the soaker fabric

Using Cloth Diapers

Please note that there are many styles and many different ideas on the construction, care, and use of cloth diapers, all of which you should explore before cloth diapering (see the resources at the back of the book for more information). What I share here is the simplest method by which I have cloth diapered three children—with ease and pleasure, I assure you—from birth to potty learning.

This pattern will make a flat, prefold diaper. You will still need to purchase a diaper cover. Cloth diaper covers have come a long way since the diaper pins and plastic pants of our youth. A wide variety of options is available—from fleece or wool to cotton or polyester. Online you will find many patterns for making your own diaper covers as well as many work-at-home, mother-owned companies that make and sell diaper covers (see the Resource Guide in the back of the book). I've used wool wraps exclusively with my little ones, and I love the breathability and comfort that wool provides.

CRAFTY TIP

For this project, due to the thickness of the fabric you'll be sewing, you will need to use a heavier needle on your sewing machine. I recommend sewing diapers with a size 14 machine needle. A serger is excellent for this project, but instructions are given for a standard sewing machine as well.

Caring for Cloth Diapers

The system that always works in my home is to give diapers a quick rinse and then store worn diapers in a diaper pail (a plastic trash can with a lid) until washday. I wash diapers with regular laundry soap in hot water followed by a cold rinse. I usually dry the diapers on the clothesline, not only for the environmental efficiency, but also for the amazing stain-removing powers of the sun. Never use bleach or harmful detergents on your baby's diapers.

1. PREPARE MATERIALS

Gather all materials and cut all fabrics to the measurements given above.

2. ASSEMBLE SOAKER FABRICS

Stack the two soaker pieces on top of each other. Place this stack in the center of one of the larger pieces of diaper fabric (right or wrong side doesn't matter as this larger piece will be the middle layer, invisible from the outside). Pin the three layers in place. Using a zigzag stitch, secure the soaker stack to the center of the larger piece with stitches down both sides of the stack, stitching as close to the raw edge as you can.

3. ASSEMBLE DIAPER

Place one large piece on a flat surface, wrong side up. Lay another large piece directly on top. Next add the large piece with the soaker attached. Last, add the final large piece, right side up. Align all four large pieces, and pin them in place.

4. FINISH DIAPER

If you have a serger, serge all four sides. If you are using a standard sewing machine, adjust the zigzag stitch to a tight setting and stitch around all four sides of the diaper, as close to the edge as you can. Repeat the zigzag stitch around the entire diaper one more time. Trim away the excess fabric, being careful to avoid cutting the stitches.

In the center of the diaper, where the soaker lies, topstitch two seams down the sides to further secure the diaper in the middle.

Repeat these steps for as many diapers as you need. I recommend a minimum of 24 diapers for a newborn's diaper collection; 36 is ideal if you want a few days between washings.

EARTHY TIP

If you'll be making cloth diapers, why not go the extra step and make a few cloth wipes? It's so simple: using old T-shirts or jersey, cut two pieces of fabric into 8″ squares and serge or zigzag them together (similar to the diaper instructions here). Wash your wipes by dipping them once into a jar or commercial baby wipes container filled with solution. My favorite recipe for diaper wipes wash is to gently mix together 1 tablespoon of Dr. Bronner's Baby Mild Liquid Soap, 1 tablespoon of almond oil, 1 drop of tea tree oil, 1 drop of lavender oil, and ¾ cup of water. Change the solution every week or so.

women's cloth

~~~~~~

*D*isposable menstrual pads have become the norm only in the past 30 years or so as a relacement to the traditional cloth, rag, fabric, or knitted pad. But today, with both a feminist and an environmental momentum, cloth pads (as well as cuplike alternatives such as The Keeper) and are being used once again with increased popularity.

Cloth menstrual pads are a wonderful option to the plastic alternatives. Cotton is soft, breathable, and comfortable in a way that plastic tampons or pads can't be, just by nature of their materials. Many women believe the use of cloth decreases their menstrual cramps and allows them to be more in tune with their body's natural rhythm. I began to use cloth when I began cloth diapering my little ones. If I was choosing cloth over plastic for them—for reasons relating to the environment, comfort, and finances—why not do the same for myself? Once I made the decision to give cloth pads a try, it only made sense that I'd make them myself.

If switching to cloth menstrual pads exclusively seems overwhelming to you, try wearing them overnight or when you are at home. When you get more comfortable wearing them, you'll be able to extend your use.

Pattern Details

Intermediate
A day project (to make several)
Finished size: 10″ × 6″ (including wings)

Use What You Have

Flannel shirts or bedsheets work very well for this project. T-shirts are also a possibility, though the stretch can make them difficult to sew. Use T-shirts if you have experience sewing with knits. (*The photographed cloth pads are made from flannel sheets and jersey shirts.*)

Materials

Approximately ½ yard total per pad, as follows:

Fabric: (3–6) 11″ × 8″ pieces
Pattern piece F (found on page 185)
Snaps and a snap setter or round Velcro tabs

A Note about the Sizing

Every woman's cycle and flow are different, so please do make one of these and try it out before you make many more. You may find that these instructions make a pad that is too thick or too thin for you. You can easily add or remove layers to design one that fits just right.

Cleaning Cloth Pads

I find it's best to rinse or soak used pads before washing (an enamel pot with a lid in the bathroom is a great solution). When your cycle is over (or before if you've run out of cloth pads), simply wash the pads with regular laundry soap in a hot wash/cold rinse cycle. Never use bleach. Dry them in the clothes dryer with your other laundry, or hang them up to line dry. The sun—just like it does for cloth diapers—will help remove any stains. If you need additional stain removal, use a natural enzyme stain remover. (Note: If you are cloth diapering, you can wash your cloth pads right along with your cloth diapers; the care for both is the same.)

1. PREPARE MATERIALS

Gather all materials and cut all fabrics to the measurements given above.

2. PREPARE PATTERN PIECES

Using pattern piece F, cut two pieces for the top and bottom of the pad and as many pieces of fabric as needed for the layers. Using a midweight flannel fabric, use three layers for light flow, use four to five layers for regular flow, use six layers for heavy flow or overnight use. (Note: You may need to adjust the number of layers according to the thickness of the fabric you choose.)

Cut the wings off all the middle layers to prevent that part of the pad from becoming too bulky.

3. ASSEMBLE PAD

Layer the pieces on top of each other in this order: bottom fabric right side up, top fabric right side down, then middle layers with right side either up or down. Pin the layers securely in place.

Starting on the side edge of one wing, stitch around the entire pad. Stop stitching when you come to the end of that same wing flap, leaving the end open for turning. Trim the seam and clip the curves and corners without clipping the stitching.

Through the wing flap opening, turn the pad right side out. Use your fingers or a turning tool to smooth out the seam. Press. On the open wing, turn the fabric toward the wrong side ¼″ and press. Place a pin here to hold the turned fabric in place.

Topstitch around the entire pad, including the wings.

4. FINISH PAD

If you have a snap, attach one half to each wing so that they will cross, overlap, and snap onto one another below your panties. If you are using Velcro, sew it on the wings following the manufacturer's instructions.

Baby Sling

~~~~~~~~~~

*I*n my opinion, the sling is among the most essential of baby gear. Our children have slept, nursed, cried, laughed, and snuggled in our slings for many hours of every day of their first year of life. It's a place of refuge for them, however brief the visit to it may be, and a spot where they can lay their heads right next to our hearts and find comfort and peace in our arms. All the while, Mama or Papa has both arms to carry on with the other needs and activities of our lives.

Pattern Details

Intermediate
An afternoon project
Finished size: Based on individual size

Use What You Have

Tablecloths make wonderful slings because they're just a bit heavier in weight, which gives them a bit more strength. Working equally well are light- to midweight bedspreads, shower curtains, soft home décor fabric, or thick bedsheets. Be sure that your chosen piece of fabric is free from holes, tears, and thin spots. While not necessary to the construction, I do believe 100-percent cotton is preferred next to babies' and parents' skin. (*The photographed sling is made from a vintage tablecloth.*)

Sizing

The sizing of a sling is very important. If the fit isn't right, the sling won't be comfortable or safe for you or your baby. Please be sure to use the sizing chart to find the proper size. The bottom seam of the sling, when finished, should sit right at your hip. Even within those general sizes, however, every body shape and type is different, and your sling may need some adjustments to fit properly. If you have doubts about which size sling to make, go a size larger; it's quite easy to shorten a sling. (See the notes at the end of this project.)

Sizing Chart

SLING SIZE BASED ON ADULT HEIGHT	FABRIC SIZE
Smaller	51″ × 22″
Average (5′6″ to 5′10″)	56″ × 22″
Larger	64″ × 22″

Materials

Approximately 2 yards, as follows:

Fabric: (1) 56″ × 22″ piece of midweight fabric for the sling (See chart for size variations.)

SIZING FOR CHILDREN

To make a doll sling for your little one, use the same instructions but change the fabric measurements to 40″ × 19″.

I. PREPARE MATERIALS

Gather all materials and cut all fabrics to the measurements given above.

2. HEM FABRIC

Fold over both long ends of the fabric piece ¼″ and press. Fold over another ½″ and press. Stitch.

3. CONSTRUCT SLING

With wrong sides together, fold the piece in half lengthwise, matching up the two shorter sides. Fold this piece once more, widthwise, so the fabric measures 28″ × 11″ (or similar, based on your size variation).

Place the fabric on a flat surface so the folded long edge is at the bottom and the raw edges are to the right. Along the top of the fabric, place a pin 4″ in from the short raw edge. Starting at the bottom raw edge corner, mark a slight curve from the corner to your marked pin. Cut along this line through all four layers of fabric.

Unfold the fabric once so you have two layers of fabric again. Keeping the wrong sides together, sew the curved edge with a ¼″ seam allowance.

4. FINISH SLING

Turn the sling wrong side out and press along the curved edge. Stitch again on the curved edge. Use a ¾″ seam allowance to envelop the first seam inside your stitching. Turn the sling right side out. (This is a French seam.)

From the inside (wrong side of fabric) of the sling, press this curved seam to one side. Use a zigzag stitch to sew the seam flat. Repeat the stitch to strengthen the sling seam.

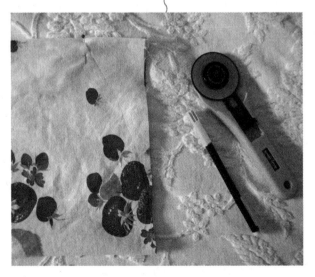

Shortening Your Sling

1. Determine the amount of shortening the sling needs by pinning and experimenting with length. Allow room for sling to stretch with the baby in it—without actually putting the baby in the sling at this point. Mark where the new seam should go.
2. Turn sling inside out, and fold it in half. Following the existing curve, draw a line in this new position. Cut along this line.
3. With wrong sides together, sew a ¼″ seam along the curved edge. Follow Step 4: Finish Sling.

Wearing Your Baby in a Sling

I cannot adequately show you how to wear your baby in a sling through the text in this book. Please be sure—by researching the methods, learning from other women, and by practicing with a doll first—that you are confident and experienced before placing a baby in the sling for the first time. We don't want any dropped babies!

It is essential for your baby's comfort and safety that a sling be worn properly. The best, and the traditional, way to learn to wear and use a sling is by watching and learning from other women. Seek out babywearers in your community. Many hospitals, birth centers, and breastfeeding support groups will have experts who will be able to assist you. Additionally, you can find many resources, instructions, and videos online for the different carrying styles. Check the resources in the back of this book for some Web sites to get you started slinging your babe.

To begin, fold the sling in half, wrong sides together so that you create a tube with a pocket. Place the sling over your head, resting it on one shoulder. The curved seam should sit at your hip.

There are many ways to hold a baby in a sling, depending on the baby's size, comfort, or your preference.

For a young baby, try the front carry: Fully open the sling pocket and gently place the baby into the pocket. Be sure one side of the fabric is between you and the baby. He or she may sit cross-legged across your belly or with his or her bottom along the seam of the sling.

For an older child (one who is able to sit up fully), try a hip carry: Place the seam of the sling fully on your side, open the pocket, and place baby's bottom on your hip and along the seam, with his or her legs out below the sling. Be sure the sling is high enough on his or her back to keep the baby secure and that there is enough fabric around the baby's bottom to hold him or her safely in the sling.

Comforts of Home

Do what you can, with what you have, where you are.

—THEODORE ROOSEVELT

Home and comfort are synonymous, aren't they? I think so. Home itself feels comforting, but so, too, do the items we keep in our homes. So many things—in each and every room—bring me comfort in times of distress and remind me of love in times of sadness.

Sometimes the children and I talk about what our favorite thing is in the house. The answer is hardly ever the same from any of us. It varies depending on our age, our mood, and our needs at the time. Often, our favorites are hand-made creations. Sometimes they are old. Always they are loved and carry with them memories and feelings of home and family.

My great grandmother's kneading board is one of my comforts. It's a simple piece of wood—a worn, old, and tired piece of wood, if the truth be told. And yet, it's one of my most treasured keepsakes. When I stand at it, kneading the bread for my family's evening meal, I feel surrounded, strengthened, and inspired by the woman I have heard so much about but never actually had the chance to meet.

Raising her children in rural Maine in the Depression, my grandmother was a mother parenting alone most of the time. Struggling to find money to feed her children, moving them often . . . This was her life. And yet the stories I hear of her are full of strong faith, great humor, and a deep love for her children.

Standing at the board today, in my own home, I think of her life and mine and how different they are. I think of how grateful I am for what I have and why I have it. But I also think about how very much we share: the anguish, the joy, the tears, and the laughter of motherhood and life.

That old saying, "It's the little things," certainly fits much of family life for me. A big birthday party, a family vacation, or other large-scale events like those are all wonderful, precious, and such a treat. But it's the day-to-day little things we do—cleaning our home and our bodies, caring for ourselves in sickness and in health, nurturing a new baby—that carry the biggest impact in our lives and the lives of our children.

One such "little thing" very dear to my family is the concept of a healing basket. In our home, the healing basket is a petite vintage picnic basket containing all the things that one might need when he or she is not feeling well. It is a first aid kit, without the medicine, so to speak. In our healing basket are a Silky Eye Pillow and Papa's Healing Cozy (two projects both found in this chapter), as well as colorful Band-Aids, a small book of meditations for children, and the bottle and recipe for our Magic Spray (see sidebar). I also include a few bits of the basic homeopathic and herbal remedies that we use in times of need: arnica, calendula, Bach Rescue Remedy, and tea tree oil.

The most important things in the basket, however, are really about connecting, slowing down, and truly being with and at the side of the one who is hurting. The healing basket is something that we can reach for in times of pain, stress, and sadness—and it's a place where our children can find comfort with our help.

MAGIC SPRAY

Magic Spray is perfect for someone with a fever who needs a bit of a cool-down or for someone with any kind of a challenge who needs a snuggle and some relaxation. To make your own Magic Spray, combine 2 cups of water and 1 drop of each of the following essential oils: rose, lavender, and chamomile. Pour it in a spray bottle and try it on yourself first to make sure the spray is more of a gentle mist. Keeping clear of the face, mist this healing spray on the arms, legs, and trunk of a hurting little one for a soothing wash.

3

Play

Projects to inspire imagination and growth

~~~~~~~~~~~~~~~~~~~~~~~~~~~~~~~~

The patterns and projects in Play are intended to inspire imagination and growth. Both of these items are essential to the heart of a creative family—for both the parents and our children, alone and together. Here you'll find activities that feature lots of parent and child collaborations, as well as projects that make the play of our day-to-day life more comfortable and more fun.

Meg's Art Tray

~~~~~~~~~

With the help of our friend, Meg Rooks (fellow mama and crafter featured on page 117 in "The Art of Play"), my little ones and I created these art trays, which include some drawings from the overflowing pile of bird drawings found in our home. The activity of writing and drawing takes place all over our home—not just at the drawing table or our dining room table. Sometimes it's fun to cozy up by the woodstove with a blanket and some hot cocoa for some drawing or to snuggle up on a bed for a cozy letter writing session. Other times, we'll take a tray of colored pencils and paper outside for a little bird drawing session. These trays have become the perfect portable way to do so.

Pattern Details

Beginner
A half-day project
Suitable for little hands

Use What You Have

This project calls for artwork in print form. Look for books at thrift shops (or on your shelves) that are too stained, old, or torn to be suitable for reading. Children's artwork is a wonderful resource as well! Breakfast trays can be found thrifted or new. (*The photographed tray is made from children's drawings decoupaged onto a thrifted metal tray.*)

Materials

Artwork to cover the desired surface (Note: If you are using children's art, be sure it is a medium that will not smudge when glue is applied. Pen, pencil, and marker usually work well. Alternatively, and to keep the original, photocopy the artwork onto copy paper.)

Decoupage glue in matte or glossy finish (Note: Purchase a premade brand such as Mod Podge).

Sponge paintbrush

Breakfast tray with a primarily flat surface

Soapy washcloth and towels for cleanup

Optional: Clear acrylic sealer

1. PREPARE MATERIALS

Gather all materials listed above and prepare an appropriate work surface. A vinyl tablecloth, cut paper grocery bags, or newspaper will all work well if you'll be working on a surface that needs to be protected.

Cut your artwork as desired. If you would like the artwork to go right to the edges of the tray, you'll need to cut some straight lines around the artwork as well as curves. Alternatively, you could lay a single layer of white copy paper as a foundation with shaped pieces on top.

Clean the art tray with soap and water and dry thoroughly.

2. APPLY GLUE

Using a sponge brush, paint the back of the first layer/piece of paper with the decoupage glue. Apply it to the tray as desired. Smooth out any wrinkles with your fingers. Apply another layer of glue on the top. Repeat step 2 with all of your artwork until the desired look is complete.

MEG'S DECOUPAGE TIPS

1. Experiment with paper and glue first to make sure the paper will work well. Stiff paper and cardstock generally don't cooperate, and tissue paper tends to fall apart.
2. Don't worry about small air bubbles; they tend to work themselves out as the glue dries. Also, remember that the glue will dry nice and clear, so don't worry if you've used a lot and your project looks messy.
3. Use a layer of glue both under and over the paper (put down some glue, slap on the paper, put more glue on top, then smooth it out).
4. After the glue has dried, apply and let dry at least two more layers of glue. The more layers you apply, the better sealed the piece will be.

3. FINISH TRAY

Let the artwork dry, and apply a coat of glue. Let it dry again, and repeat the applications of glue until the art tray is finished as desired. If the art tray will be washed, spray it with an acrylic sealer.

CRAFTY TIP

You can make your own decoupage glue by mixing equal parts of white glue and water. Add more glue or water as needed to create a smooth, paintlike consistency.

Brandie's Book

A scrapbooker, letter writer, photographer, magazine lover, and journaler, our friend Brandie created these unique handmade journals out of all the piles of paper in her home. She customizes each for the intended recipient—mostly her three journal-loving daughters. She personalizes them by including their favorite colors; bits of their papers; favorite cards, photographs, and letters; and so much more. Amidst all this special paper are blank pages for their own writing and drawing. My first sight of these journals sent me straight home to my recycling bin and then the paper cutter!

Because these books are highly customizable, I'm sure you'll come up with lots of other sources for paper and ideas to make each journal uniquely yours. They're a great way to share a love of recycling and journaling in a personal, ecological, and creative fun way.

Pattern Details

Beginner
A half-day project
Suitable for little hands
Finished size: 7″ × 9″ or whatever size you desire

Use What You Have

You'll need a thick, heavy paper or cardboard for the outside of your journal, but not as thick as a hardcover book, as most copy centers cannot bind this thickness. Some materials that work well include book cover dust jackets, cardboard, mailers, folders, magazine covers, paperback book covers, cardboard food boxes, and so much more. For the inside pages, try a mix of light- and midweight papers. Some materials that work well include discarded book pages, recycled paper, receipts, tags, magazine and catalog clippings, envelopes, postcards, cards, photographs, letters, calendar pages, children's art, wrapping paper, and unlined, lined, or graph paper for the blank pages. The possibilities for paper sources are endless! *(The photographed books are made from a combination of materials from the above lists.)*

Materials

Paper 1: (2) 7″ × 9″ pieces of heavyweight paper for the covers
Paper 2: Many 6½″ × 8″ or smaller pieces of lightweight paper for the inside pages, using a mixture of patterned and blank pages (see above for source ideas)
Paper cutter with a ruler
Binder clip
Spiral coil binding (available at a local print shop)

I. PREPARE MATERIALS

Gather all materials, selecting the papers you'll use for your book cover and interior pages.

2. MAKE BOOK COVER

Begin by cutting two pieces of the book cover paper to 7″ × 9″. These will be your front and back book covers. (*Note:* Your book can be any size you want, but for the purposes of these instructions, this journal will be 7″ × 9″.)

3. CUT INTERIOR PAGES

Once you have selected the size of your book and have cut your front and back covers, it's time to determine the measurements for the inside paper. I like to leave nearly ½″ of cover around three edges of the book; the fourth side will have a binding. So, for a book that measures 7″ × 9″, the inside page measurements will be 6½″ × 8″.

Cut the inside pages to 6½″ × 8″. Many of your pieces may be smaller than this, but don't worry—the pages are not intended to be the same size. Just make sure that the inside pages aren't larger than the inside page measurement (6½″ × 8″).

4. ARRANGE INTERIOR PAGES

After the paper is cut and you have as many pages as you would like (approximately ³⁄₄″ is a good thickness), you can begin to sort the pages into a desired order. I like to have the blank paper evenly distributed throughout the book, interspersed by other kinds of printed paper.

5. FINISH BOOK

Very carefully, align the pages to the left side, where the binding will be. Place a binder clip—or several—on this side to keep the pages in place.

Take your book pages to a local print and copy shop to request a spiral coil binding.

Ezra's Letter Satchel

~~~~~~~~~~

*W*hile our family tries hard to reduce our consumption of paper, we also place great value on the tradition of letter writing. There's something so methodical, mindful, and real about connecting with loved ones through the handwritten word.

My children love to write letters as much as I do. My son Ezra has a few pen pals, and he treasures the letters he receives from them, saving them in a bundle to sit down and read all at once. Together we came up with this letter satchel: a way for him to store and carry all of his letters so he can indulge in a leisurely read whenever his little letter-loving heart desires. Because it's a project the children can be quite involved in making, the satchel has since become a favorite child-friendly gift. And what person doesn't need a satchel for all his or her special letters?

Pattern Details

Beginner
A half-day project
Suitable for little hands
Finished size: 11″ × 7½″

Use What You Have

Nearly all cotton or wool fabrics will work for this project. A heavier weight fabric is best for the outside piece, while the inside lining can be made with a lighter weight fabric, if desired. *(The photographed satchel is made from scrap twill fabric for the outside, a cotton bedsheet scrap for the inside, and a wool blanket scrap for the label.)*

Materials

Approximately 1 yard total, as follows:

Fabric 1: (1) 20″ × 12″ piece for the outside
Fabric 2: (1) 20″ × 12″ piece for the lining
Fabric 3: (1) 2″ × 4″ piece of white fabric for the lettered label
Lightweight fusible interfacing: (1) 20″ × 12″
Masking tape
Fabric marker
Velcro circles: (2) ½″ diameter
Button: (1) ½″ wide or larger
Optional: Embroidery floss, needle, and small 3″ hoop

I. PREPARE MATERIALS

Gather all materials and cut all fabrics to the measurements given above.

2. MAKE LETTERED FABRIC

Tape the white (or light-colored) small fabric piece to a flat surface. Using the fabric marker and following the manufacturer's instructions, have your child (or yourself) write the desired word on the strip. At this point, if desired, you can embroider over the lettering with embroidery floss.

3. ATTACH LETTERED FABRIC TO FLAP

Lay the outside fabric flat, right side up and vertically on your work surface. Place the lettered fabric in the bottom center, about 1 1/2″ up from the bottom 12″-long edge. Pin it in place. This will be the flap.

Using a zigzag stitch, stitch around all four sides of your lettered piece, securing it to the fabric.

4. PREPARE FLAP

Following the manufacturer's instructions, attach the interfacing to the wrong side of the lining fabric. Place the lining and the outside fabric right sides together and pin all four sides. Lay the pinned pieces on the work surface so the wrong side of the outside fabric is facing up. The 12″ end where you attached the lettered piece should be at the bottom.

On that 12″ end, measure 1″ from the left corner toward the bag's center at a 45-degree angle and mark a dot. With this dot as your center point, draw a straight line from one edge of the fabric to the other, creating a triangle at the tip of the corner. Cut this tip off the larger piece of fabric, cutting through the outside fabric, interfacing, and lining. Repeat this process on the left corner, using the cut triangle as a template.

5. SEW OUTSIDE AND LINING TOGETHER

Starting in the middle of either long side, begin to stitch a seam. Stitch around all four sides (and corners) of the piece, stopping 3″ before reaching your starting point.

Trim the corners without cutting through the stitches. Turn the sewn pieces right side out through the 3″ opening. Press.

6. SEW SATCHEL

Lay the entire satchel flat on your work surface with the lining facing up and the flap end at the top. Bring up the bottom edge of the satchel, folding it 4″ below the top edge to create a pocket. Pin the material in place.

Using a zigzag stitch, sew down both sides of the satchel pocket, being sure to reinforce it with extra stitching at both ends.

7. FINISH SATCHEL

Sew Velcro circles on the wrong side of the flap and the right side of the pocket in corresponding spots.

Sew a button to the front of the flap, as a decorative element to cover the stitches for the Velcro.

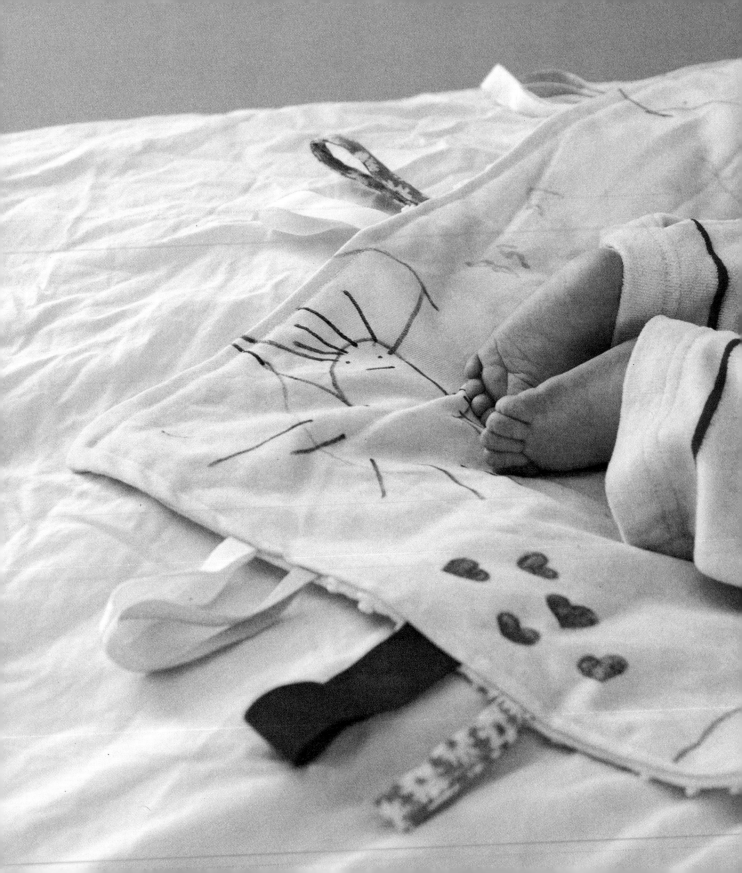

baby's fringed play mat

*W*hen a new little one enters the world in our circle of friends or family, my little ones are just as excited to greet them as we are. I'm always looking for ways to include them in this welcoming process, either through the baking of food for the family, the expressions of love in cards and drawings, or the making of gifts for the new baby.

This play mat evolved as a handmade gift that the whole family could create and give to a newborn. My children love dreaming up the artwork that should be on each baby's play mat, giving careful thought and consideration to the interests of the family, the time of year in which the baby is born, and the other elements of the new one's life.

Pattern Details

Intermediate
A weekend project
Suitable for little hands
Finished size: 35″ × 35″

Use What You Have

Most 100-percent cotton fabrics will work well for the top of this play mat; quilting cottons and vintage bedsheets are wonderful. Choose a light-colored fabric for the top—preferably white, cream, or a pastel—so the artwork of your little one will show well. The back of the play mat can be made from a thicker fabric: bedspreads, soft upholstery fabric, wool blankets, or flannel. For batting, use quilt cotton batting or a large beach towel. The fringe strips are an excellent way to use up fabric scraps. I prefer to use 100-percent cottons on all three blanket layers when making a gift for baby. (*The photographed play mat is made from a vintage bedsheet for the top, a vintage chenille bedspread for the back, and vintage and new ribbon scraps for the fringe.*)

Materials

Approximately 2 yards total, as follows:

Fabric 1: (1) 36″ × 36″ piece for the top
Fabric 2: (1) 36″ × 36″ piece for the bottom
Ribbon: (24) in varying lengths between 6″ and 8″
Quilt batting: (1) 36″ × 36″
Fabric markers

I. PREPARE MATERIALS

Gather all materials and cut all fabrics to the measurements given above.

2. CREATE ARTWORK FOR TOP

Begin by using the fabric markers to draw the artwork on the top layer. I find it easiest to tape the top fabric to the floor or table. Follow the manufacturer's instructions for specifics on washing, applying, and drying times.

3. MAKE RIBBON FRINGE

Fold a length of ribbon in half lengthwise. To attach the fringe, lay the play mat top flat, right side up. Place the ribbons on the play mat top: the raw edges of the ribbons should be aligned with the raw edge of the play mat and the folded edge of the ribbons should face the center of the blanket. (When you complete the blanket, the fringe will be on the outside.) Pin and baste each ribbon in place $1/8''$ from the raw edge.

4. ASSEMBLE PLAY MAT

First, lay the bottom fabric flat, right side up, being sure to smooth out all the wrinkles. On top of that, lay the top fabric, right side down, so the top and bottom right sides are together. The fringes will disappear between the two layers. Add the batting to the top of the stack. Pin around the edges of the play mat, including a few pins in the middle to hold the pieces in place while you sew.

Beginning at the halfway point on one side, stitch all three pieces together around the entire blanket, stopping $4''$ before your starting point to leave an opening. Trim the seam and clip the corners, being careful to avoid cutting the stitches.

Reach through the opening between the top and the bottom of the blanket to turn the blanket inside out. Using your fingers, push out all four corners. Press the entire play mat smooth.

5. FINISH PLAY MAT

Topstitch ½" in around all of the edges. Be careful to keep the fringe out of the way and pointing away from the blanket. Continue around all sides of the blanket, closing the opening with your stitches as you go.

To quilt your play mat, stitch a square through all the thicknesses of the play mat 4" inside the topstitched square you just created. Repeat the stitching one more time inside that square for a total of three stitched squares, including the original topstitching.

cozy wall pockets

~~~~~~~~~

*W*ith three little ones at home, we're always in need of more nooks and crannies in which to place all the tools of creativity that go along with their play. This wall pocket is one solution we came up with to keep an area tidy and free of clutter. Using a wool blanket as a base fabric adds a real element of softness and comfort to the whole project, giving it the ability to transform an area into a cozy little nook for playing, dreaming, reading, and snuggling.

Pattern Details

Intermediate
A day project
Suitable for help from little hands
Finished size: 35″ × 38″

Use What You Have

Wool blankets are the ideal material for this project. Look for 100-percent wool blankets, vintage or new. Because of the small size of the pocket panel, this project provides an excellent use for a blanket with stains, tears, or discoloration. If wool blankets are not an option for you, wool fabric will also work well. Look for suiting fabric at your local fabric shop. Any light- to midweight fabric is ideal for the pockets. (*The photographed wall pocket is made from a thrifted wool blanket for the main panel and cotton fabrics for the pockets.*)

Materials

Approximately 1½ yards of wool and 2 yards of pocket fabric total, as follows:

Fabric 1: (1) 35″ × 38″ piece of wool for the main panel
Fabric 2: (1) 36″ × 12″, (1) 11″ × 7″, and (1) 24″ × 10″ pieces of fabric for 3 printed pockets
Fabric 3: (1) 10″ × 10″ piece of solid fabric for 1 pocket
Fabric pencil
Embroidery needle and floss
Masking tape
Embroidered ribbon or twill tape: (6) 10″ strips
1″-thick fallen tree branch or wooden dowel: (1) 42″ long
Buttons: (6) ½″ diameter or larger
Pinking shears
Nails or hooks for hanging finished project

1. PREPARE MATERIALS

Gather all materials and cut all fabrics to the measurements given above.

2. PREPARE FABRICS

Use pinking shears to trim the wool blanket for a zigzag finish.

Prepare all four of the pocket pieces as follows: With the wrong side of fabric facing up, fold over the top edge of the piece 1/4" toward the center of the pocket. Press. Fold again 1/2". Press. Machine stitch a hem on this fold. On the remaining three edges, fold each edge 1/4" toward the center of the pocket. Press. Fold again 1/4". Press. Set the fabric pockets aside.

EARTHY TIP

Natural plants make an excellent source of dyes that work beautifully on wool, so you can use them to turn a basic white or ivory wool blanket into any color in the natural world! Check out *Natural Dyes* by Linda Rudkin or look in the resources for additional references.

3. EMBROIDER SOLID POCKET

At this point, have your little ones (and you!) draw on the white fabric pockets with a fabric pencil. I find it helpful to use masking tape to secure the fabric to a table to keep the fabric taut while the children are drawing. Using three strands of embroidery floss, embroider over the pencil markings (slip stitch, backstitch, or split stitch all work well for outlines such as these).

4. ATTACH POCKETS

Arrange all of the pockets on the wool panel, making sure the stitched 1/2" hem is on the top, and adjust the placement as desired. Pin the pockets in place. Sew the pockets to the blanket by stitching 1/8" from the left, right, and bottom edges of each pocket. Be sure to backstitch well at the top corner of each side.

You can divide the pockets into smaller sections at this point by marking and stitching a straight vertical line through any pocket. Smaller sections are particularly useful in the wide pockets. Think about what will be placed in each pocket, measure the item, and sew an appropriately sized slot.

5. FINISH WALL POCKETS

Along the top edge of the blanket and beginning 1" in from a side edge, measure and mark five evenly spaced points across the top.

Attach rod loops as follows: Place the bottom edge of a piece of ribbon 1″ below the top edge of the wool panel, with one side of the ribbon on each side of panel. Pin the ribbon in place. Machine stitch a wide zigzag from the top of the wool panel down to the bottom of the ribbon to secure the ribbon in place. Be sure to stitch through all three layers: bottom ribbon, wool panel, and top ribbon. Place and sew the buttons on top of the ribbon to hide the stitch marks.

Slide the tree branch or wooden dowel through the ribbon loops so the panel hangs evenly. Hang the wall pockets from the wall (or door) with nails or hooks.

portrait bookmarks

~~~~~~~~~~

*T*he drawings my children make of people are so very dear to me. All along in their learning process—from the earliest of blobs (in which I look quite like a potato spud) to the later years when the details of fingers and toes and hair are added—I'm intrigued and in love with the portraits they create of those they love. I'm always so impressed at the elements of personality they manage to convey in their portraits despite their young years and new drawing skills.

These portrait bookmarks evolved like many projects do in our home: out of a need for bookmarks to keep our places in all the books around our house and out of a desire to save and treasure our children's interpretations of each other at these important moments in their lives.

Pattern Details

Intermediate
A day project
Suitable for little hands
Finished size: $3\frac{1}{2}'' \times 7\frac{1}{2}''$

Use What You Have

This project is excellent for using up scraps that you may have, since the pieces needed are so small. Nearly any midweight cotton fabric will do—from bedsheets to linen to quilting cotton. You'll likely want a light color to work well with the embroidery. (*The photographed bookmarks are made from linen scraps for the front, vintage fabric scraps for the back, and vintage ribbon trim for the top loop.*)

Materials

Approximately $\frac{1}{2}$ yard total, as follows:

Fabric 1: (1) $9'' \times 9''$ piece for bookmark front
Fabric 2: (1) $8'' \times 4''$ piece for bookmark back
Lightweight fusible interfacing: (1) $8'' \times 4''$
Ribbon: $5''$ long
Embroidery needle and floss
$6''$ embroidery hoop
Masking tape

1. PREPARE MATERIALS

Gather all materials and cut all fabrics to the measurements given above.

2. DRAW BOOKMARK PORTRAIT

Use a pencil to mark an 8″ × 4″ rectangle in the center of the 9″ × 9″ front fabric. (*Note:* Eventually the fabric will be cut along these lines, but it starts out larger to accommodate an embroidery hoop.)

Use masking tape to secure this larger fabric square to a hard surface. Ask your child to draw a portrait inside the marked lines for the rectangle. When drawing, allow at least a ½″ margin between the drawing and the line. If your child is too young for this specific instruction, use additional masking tape to further clarify the drawing area. When the portrait is complete, add any additional words, names, or information on the bookmark.

3. EMBROIDER DRAWING

Remove the tape from the fabric, and place the piece inside an embroidery hoop with the drawing in the center. Using a simple backstitch (described on page 21) and all six strands of embroidery floss, follow the outline of your child's drawing. Adjust the fabric in the hoop as needed to reach all the drawings and letters.

Remove the fabric from the hoop, and cut along all four sides of the marked rectangle. You now have an 8″ × 4″ bookmark front. Set this piece aside.

4. ADHERE INTERFACING TO BACK FABRIC

With a hot iron, and following the instructions for the interfacing, adhere the interfacing to the wrong side of the back fabric piece.

5. ASSEMBLE BOOKMARK

On a flat surface, lay the back fabric piece right side up. On top of this, place the front fabric piece right side down. The two right sides of the bookmark pieces are now together. Pin the pieces in place.

6. SEW BOOKMARK

Start sewing along the top edge of the bookmark, 1″ away from the corner. Machine stitch ¼″ from the edge. Continue around all four sides, stopping 1″ past the opposite corner on the top edge, leaving a 2″ opening at the top center.

Cut the tip off all four corners, being careful to avoid cutting the stitches. These cuts will make the corner points more distinct.

Through the 2″ opening at the top, turn the bookmark right side out. Work slowly and pull gently. Use a chopstick or pencil to carefully push out the four corners. Press.

7. FINISH BOOKMARK

Fold the ribbon in half to make a loop. Place this loop inside the 2″ opening on the bookmark, approximately ¾″ into the bookmark. Pin the loop in place.

Stitch around all four sides of the bookmark, double stitching the top edge to securely fasten the ribbon to the bookmark.

art and hooks rack

~~~~~~~~~~

*I*n my home—and I'm quite sure in yours, too—there is no shortage of children's artwork. Also in my home, there is no shortage of bags, hats, sweaters, and other things that require hanging. This project is a great way to do something special with all that artwork we love, while also creating a place to hang all the many things that go along with family life at home. It's a little bit of art and function together in one versatile piece that your little ones—and you—will love.

Pattern Details

Intermediate
A day project
Suitable for little hands
Finished size: $24^1/_2'' \times 12'' \times 1''$

Use What You Have

This project calls for a piece of hardwood. Found wood, scrap wood, or salvaged wood is perfect for this project. The wood panel can be any size you desire. A smooth surface that will hold paint and glue well is the only essential. The panel should be at least $1/_2''$ in thickness to accommodate the screws. *(The photographed rack is made from a scrap piece of birch wood, 1" thick, 24" wide, and 12" high.)*

Materials

Wood panel: 1 found, scrap, repurposed, or salvaged panel of wood in any size
3–6 hooks or knobs depending on the size of your wood panel
Sandpaper
1 quart of water-based paint (see page 110 for suggestions)
Paintbrush
Ribbon or embroidered trim, the length of your wood panel
Children's artwork
Decoupage glue
Paintbrush for glue
Hot glue or any other kind of heavy-duty glue
Self-leveling saw tooth hangers and nails (for hanging the finished rack)
Screwdriver
Hammer

1. PREPARE MATERIALS

Gather all materials and cut the wood to the desired size. If necessary, use sandpaper to even out any rough spots.

2. DECORATE WOOD PANEL

Paint the entire piece of wood—front, back, and all sides. Let the paint dry. Apply a second coat, if desired.

Determine the placement of the artwork, ribbon, and hooks by using the size of the artwork as a guide. Lay the artwork on the panel, and then measure and mark a straight line where you want to place the ribbon that will separate the art and the hooks.

Adjust the artwork on the board as desired, cutting the artwork as needed. Once you've decided on the layout of the artwork, begin to apply the artwork to the panel. With a paintbrush, apply a thin layer of glue to the back of the art. Place it on the panel, and smooth out any wrinkles. Repeat this process for each piece of artwork until the top portion of the panel is covered from the pencil line to the top of the board and across. Apply one final layer of glue over the entire top half of the panel. Let the glue dry.

EARTHY TIP

Instead of using traditional commercial paint products, search out a green option. Milk Paint is an environmentally safe and nontoxic alternative to common acrylic or latex paints. Made the old-fashioned way with crushed limestone, this natural paint is an inexpensive, durable, and safe option. Milk Paint also has more variation in color, lending itself well to do-it-yourself projects like this one. You can find them at www.milkpaint.com.

3. ATTACH RIBBON

Place the ribbon over the pencil mark, covering the edges of the artwork. Wrap the ribbon around the edges of the wood panel about $1/2''$ onto the back. Attach by adhering glue to the backside, and placing ribbon in place firmly. Let the glue dry.

4. FINISH ART AND HOOKS RACK

Turn the board over so the back is facing up. Position hangers where desired, and attach them with nails.

On the front of the board, arrange the hooks and then use a pencil to mark their placement. Screw the hooks to the board as marked.

Hang your rack on a wall, being sure to secure it safely in a stud or with sheetrock screws.

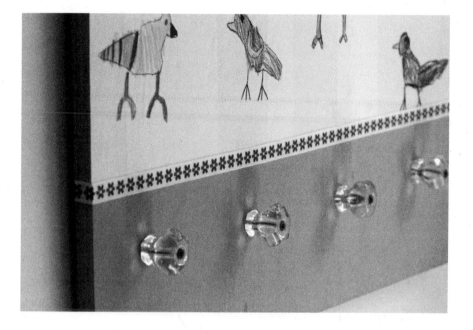

MOUSE PAD

~~~~~~~

*T*he computer—an essential piece of technology in our home—doesn's necessarily fit with the aesthetic of the rest of our home. In my opinion, a little bit of handmade—something soft and warm—can go a long way to softening up a piece of much needed and much loved technology.

This Mouse Pad was created with that softness in mind. Not only does it serve a specific function, but it also gives me a tiny way to add a little bit of handmade where it might not otherwise be found. And it's a fabulous way to showcase the tiny little piece of your favorite fabric print—in this case, feedsack.

Pattern Details

Beginner
A half-day project
Finished size: 9″ × 9″

Use What You Have

This project conveniently uses up almost any type of small fabric pieces. Cotton is best, so quilting cotton, linen, duck, and even cotton upholstery-weight fabrics all work wonderfully here. The strip of contrasting fabric along the edge of the pad makes a great place to put a favorite piece of fabric you'd like to really savor and see regularly. *(The photographed mouse pad is made from linen and fabric scraps.)*

Materials

Approximately ¼ yard total, as follows:

Fabric 1: (1) 9″ × 9″ piece of fabric for the back
Fabric 2: (1) 9″ × 6½″ piece of fabric for the front
Fabric 3: (1) 9″ × 3½″ piece of contrasting fabric for the front strip
Heavyweight fusible interfacing: (2) 9″ × 9″

1. PREPARE MATERIALS

Gather all materials and cut all fabrics to the measurements given above.

2. PIECE TOP

Lay the two front fabric pieces right sides together, matching up their 9″ edges. Stitch. Press the seam open.

3. ADHERE INTERFACING

Following the manufacturer's instructions, adhere the interfacing to the wrong side of the front piece that you just created. Then adhere a second piece to the wrong side of the back fabric piece.

4. FINISH MOUSE PAD

Square up these two pieces, wrong sides together, and trim away any excess. Use a tight zigzag stitch around all four sides close to the edge.

Trim as needed, being careful to avoid cutting the stitches.

The Art of Play

*If we are peaceful, if we are happy, we can smile and blossom
like a flower, and everyone in our family, our entire society,
will benefit from our peace.*

—THICH NHAT HANH

For many of us, our childhoods—and those of our parents—were spent engaged in a great deal of play: outside play in the neighborhood; imaginary play; role playing; and solitary play in the forms of writing, reading, building, and crafting.

The unfortunate truth is that we are busier today than we ever have been in the past; and while that likely won't change, we can fit in a little more time for play. Turning the television, computers, and video games off for a bit; saying yes to the activities that are most important to us and no to those that aren't; and just generally slowing life down some are little things that have the power to make a world of difference in the amount of playtime we have for our children, by ourselves, and together as a family. During these simple times of play and creating together we can connect so deeply to each other, build our relationships with one another, and strengthen our family bonds.

Of course, children aren't the only ones who need to play more. We need to play more, too, as adults, as parents, as teachers to our little ones. I've seen over and over again, in both my own life and the lives of my peers, how we as parents are so often inspired by and led to living a more playful life because of our children. What a gift they give us! This same gift leads many of us to discover a creative passion. I know I'm not the only mama who found her way to crafting when motherhood began and became a better mama because of it.

In addition to the joy and fun of crafting for our little ones, creative parents share another sentiment about crafting. Particularly in the early years of parenting, in a role filled with lots of intangible and abstract (albeit very important) tasks such as the care and love of our children, crafting becomes something tangible at the end of our days. Later it serves as a reminder of how our days were spent and a record of our time. Craft projects made while my children were little evoke a flood of memories of what was going on around me during our days at home: the laughter, the fun, the joy, and the challenges, all from a little craft project and a little time spent playing.

Artist and crafter Meg Rooks of Portland, Maine, (www.pixiegenne.typepad.com) found this to be true for herself as well. As a stay-at-home mother to two young children, she caught the crafting bug when her children were young. She says that at the end of the day-to-day work of mothering, she found pleasure and satisfaction in the tangible results of arts and crafts. Beginning with knitting, rug hooking, and decoupage, she tried any and all new craft mediums she could get her hands on. Never limiting herself to just one thing, Meg often found that a haul home from the thrift store or a rummage sale would launch a whole new craft medium for her, as she was inspired by the treasures she brought home, and the arts and crafts of generations before her.

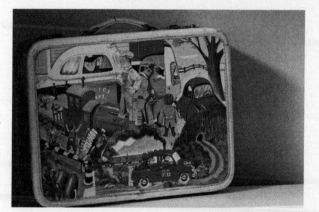

Now, with her children in school and having found her way back to her work as a children's librarian, Meg continues to find ways to weave the play of arts and crafts into her days and into the life of her family. As a master of decoupage and a lover of vintage children's book illustrations, Meg often combines the two in her work to create all sorts of useable and fun things for the home—for children and adults alike. (See Meg's Art Tray on page 85 for a project inspired by this crafty mama!) Old, vintage suitcases are transformed into works of art with a bit of paper and glue. Pails, trays, and paper goods are among her many amazing creations, and all are sources of play, pleasure, and fun.

Perhaps you, too, have been led to crafting since becoming a parent. Or perhaps it's been in you all along and now you're finding ways to fit it into your family life. Either way, it's important that we all remember to play. Watching and being inspired by our uninhibited little ones can lead us in all manner of wonderful, creative, and different directions if we're open to following them.

4

Seek

Projects to inspire
Adventure and Exploration

~~~~~~~~~~~~~~~~~~~~~~~~~~~~~~~~~~~~~~~

The patterns and projects in Seek are intended to inspire
adventure and exploration—everything from a spontane-
ous family adventure to a solo mama outing or a grand
family escapade. When we leave our home, we take our
family heart with us, and these projects are created with a
little bit of heart for the road.

Mama's Bag

~~~~~~~

I'm sure I'm not the only mama who has found herself ready for a solo outing—a little mama recharge time—and then realizes halfway out the door that the diaper bag is on her shoulder! Every mama needs a special little bag for her things, for a solo trip out or for carrying along on a road trip.

I began making this particular style of bag a few years ago, and it continues to be one of my favorite styles. It's deceptively simple in its construction, which is much like a standard tote but with a few pleats to give it a little bit of an extra kick. And the size is just right for all the essential solo mama needs. The use of vintage curtains or drapery conveys just the right amount of retro goodness without being overwhelming.

Pattern Details

Intermediate
A half-day project
Finished size: 18″ × 10″

Use What You Have

Curtains are an excellent source of fabric for repurposing. An upholstery-weight fabric makes wonderful handbags because it gives just that little bit of extra strength without interfacing or a fabric stiffener. Avoid vintage drapery with a plastic feel on the back; the plastic is very difficult to sew and can burn under an iron. Most heavyweight and home décor fabrics will work for this project. *(The photographed bags are made from vintage curtain panels with wool blanket pieces for the straps.)*

Materials

Approximately 1½ yards, as follows:

Fabric 1: (1) 19″ × 22″ piece of heavyweight fabric for the outside
Fabric 2: (1) 19″ × 22″ piece lightweight fabric for the lining
Fabric 3: (2) 4″ × 24″ pieces for the straps
Ribbon or embroidered trim: (2) 8″ long

1. PREPARE MATERIALS

Gather all materials and cut all fabrics to the measurements given above.

2. MAKE PLEATS

Along both 19″ raw edges of the outside fabric, measure and use a pin to mark points at 3″ and 6″ in from the outside edge on both sides. You should have a total of eight pins on the fabric, four on each of the 19″ edges.

Use the point of the pin to create a pleat (fold), pointed in the direction of the bag's center, 1/2″ in width. Press and pin the pleat in place. Repeat for all eight points along both sides, being sure to keep the pleats facing toward the center of the bag.

Machine baste along both edges to keep the pleats in place, removing the pins as you go.

3. PREPARE LINING

Fold the lining fabric in half, right sides together, aligning the two 19″ edges at the top. Fold the outside fabric in the same way, right sides together, with the pleated edges along the top. Place the outer fabric directly on top of the lining fabric. Using the outer fabric as a template, cut away the excess fabric along the sides of the lining fabric. Set the lining fabric aside.

4. SEW OUTSIDE FABRIC AND LINING

Beginning with the outer fabric, sew a seam down both sides. Repeat this process for the lining. Trim the corners and press the seams open on both the lining and the outer pieces.

5. MAKE STRAPS

To create the straps, first fold the fabric in half lengthwise. Press to create a crease, and then open the fabric back up. Fold again lengthwise, this time bringing each long side into the middle crease. Press. Keeping those two folds in place, fold the fabric again on the first fold, making a strap that is 1″ wide by 24″ long. Repeat this process for the second strap.

Stitch along all four sides of each strap.

6. ATTACH STRAPS

Working with the outer fabric right side out, center one end of one strap between the two pleats on the left-hand side and the other end of that same strap between the two pleats on the right-hand side. The raw edges of the bag and the strap should meet evenly, and the strap should face down toward the fold in the bag. Be sure the strap is not twisted, and pin it in place. Turn the bag over and repeat the process for the second strap. Machine baste the straps in place. (*Note:* The straps lie on the outside (right side) of the bag.)

7. ATTACH RIBBON

Along the raw edge of the top of the outside of the bag, measure and mark the exact center point between the side seams. Place the length of ribbon here, with one edge even with the raw edge of bag (as you did with the straps) and the rest of the ribbon facing down toward the bottom of the bag. Stitch the ribbon in place. Repeat the process to attach the second ribbon to the opposite side.

8. FINISH BAG

With the outer bag as it is (right side out), and the lining bag wrong side out, place the outer bag inside the lining bag and smooth it out. The right sides of the outside fabric and lining will now be facing each other, and the straps and ribbon will be sandwiched between the two right sides of the fabric. Adjust and line up the edges of both pieces so the side seams meet. Pin the pieces in place at several points along the top edge, being sure the ribbon and straps are pointed down and out of the way of the top edge.

Starting 1 1/2″ in from one of the side seams, stitch the top edge of the bag around the entire bag, stopping 1 1/2″ before the side seam where you started.

Pull the lining through the 3″ opening until it is right side out. Then push the lining inside the outer bag so the right side of lining forms the inside of the bag. Press.

Topstitch along the entire top edge of the bag, closing the 3″ opening you used to turn the bag right side out. Backstitch over the straps and ribbon to secure them in place.

Treasure Bag

~~~~~~~~~~

*I*t seems that we can't leave the beach, the woods, the park, or any other kind of outing without at least one acorn, rock, stick, or shell accompanying us home. We always try to keep our collections to a minimum, and we avoid it altogether in places where it isn't allowed. But for the most part, I think a tiny bit of treasure seeking is a good thing; these little bits of nature teach us so very much about the object itself, the environment from which it came, and the animals and creatures related to it. They become a tool for learning, just as much as they become a piece of art, or a toy, or an enjoyable piece of beauty in a bowl.

As I was changing out the screens in our windows one day, I realized the mesh would be the perfect solution for a bag that could get wet, stay wet, and filter out some of the sand and dirt that are inevitably collected along with our treasures. Now, these handy bags accompany us on many adventures to the beach, forest, and hills. Each time we head out, the bag ends up carrying a few more treasures, gathered and saved, for poring over and treasuring once home.

Pattern Details

Intermediate
A half-day project
Suitable for little hands
Finished size: 9″ × 9″

Use What You Have

This project calls for the use of a discarded window screen—a wonderful way to find another use for something that might likely have gone in the garbage otherwise. As an alternative, mesh fabric from your fabric store will also work well. *(The photographed treasure bag is made from used, soft, vinyl window screening, linen scraps for the patch, and old belt webbing for the straps.)*

Materials

Approximately 1 yard of fabric, as follows:

Fabric 1: (1) 11″ × 22″ piece of window screening or mesh
Fabric 2: (1) 7″ × 7″ piece of scrap fabric
Fabric 3: (1) 2″ × 5″ piece of linen or white fabric for the patch
Fabric paint
Alphabet rubber stamps
Extra-wide double-fold bias tape: (1) 21″ long
Webbing, ribbon, or straps: (2) 16″ long

I. PREPARE MATERIALS

Gather all materials and cut all fabrics to the measurements given above.

2. MAKE FABRIC PANEL

Prepare the linen patch by stamping your chosen word onto it with fabric paint. Let the paint dry following the manufacturer's directions.

Pin the finished linen piece directly in the middle of the fabric scrap. Stitch it in place, with your stitches ¼" in from the fabric edge. Place this fabric panel on the window screening, 3" down from one of the shorter ends and centered horizontally so that it is approximately 2" away from the left and right sides. Sew the fabric panel in place using a zigzag stitch, close to the fabric edge.

3. SEW BAG

Fold the screen rectangle in half, right sides together, and pin it in place. Stitch along the two sides, using a regular ⅝" seam allowance. Stitch again to secure.

Turn the bag right side out.

4. FINISH BAG

Beginning in the back center along the top edge, use a zigzag stitch to attach the double-fold bias to the top of the bag, thereby securing the raw edge of the window screening. Zigzag along the entire top of the bag, overlapping slightly at the beginning of your stitching.

Fold over the short edges of the ribbon or webbing ½" to cover the

EARTHY TIP

In many locations, you can find quality used surplus and salvage building and woodworking materials at retail stores dedicated to recycling. Habitat for Humanity has many retail stores under the name ReStore where you can find affordable, local, and environmentally sound materials for your next project. Go to www.habitat.org.

raw edges. Attach one strap 2″ in from the each side of the front of the bag. Stitch the strap in place with a zigzag stitch, and repeat the stitching to hold it securely in place to the bag top. Repeat the process for the strap on the back.

Beach Blanket to Go

~~~~~~~~~~

*H*ere, during our long and cold Maine winters, there is much dreaming of spring, summer, and fall days to be spent outside. Among my most treasured summer memories are the picnics of my past, as well as the picnics of today, full of small children running about, Frisbees, and sand in the toes.

Sharing food with those we love in the open air is a ritual to be celebrated. Our leisurely picnics spent by the shore of a favorite beach, on the crest of a mountaintop after a long morning hike, or during a sunny afternoon in our local city park are all connected, quite literally, by the threads of this blanket. Our picnic beach blanket is one of my most treasured handmade things, made special by the time we spend on it each and every year. I thoroughly enjoy this blanket—and it's also my favorite blanket to give. Variations of this picnic blanket have made their way into the hands of many friends (particularly as a wedding gift), and therefore, onto the shores of many more beaches than I could imagine.

Pattern Details

Advanced
A weekend project
Finished size: 59″ × 59″

Use What You Have

This picnic blanket lends itself well to the use of vintage linens and bedsheets. Bedspreads, thicker chenille, or matelasse works wonderfully for the back, giving it just a bit more weight than the front piece. (*The photographed blanket is made from vintage bedsheets for the top panel and a vintage and thrifted bedspread for the back.*)

Materials

Approximately 5 yards, as follows

Fabric 1: (1) 60″ × 60″ piece of heavyweight fabric for the back
Fabric 2: (10) 30″ × 12 ¼″ pieces of lightweight fabric for the top
Double-fold bias tape: (4) 60″ long and (2) 37″ long

I. PREPARE MATERIAL

Gather all materials and cut all fabrics to the measurements given above.

2. PIECE TOP

Lay out your 10 pieces of top fabric in two columns of five pieces, placing them as you would like them to appear on the blanket. Sew one column of five pieces together with a $1/4''$ seam allowance between each piece. Repeat this process for the second column. Press the seams open.

Sew the two rows together to create the blanket top, using a $1/4''$ seam allowance. Press the center seam open.

3. BASTE BLANKET

Lay the bottom piece flat on the floor wrong side up, smoothing out all of the wrinkles. Depending on the weight of the fabric, you may need to tape each corner to the floor to keep the fabric taut.

Center the top of the quilt, right side up, on top of the bottom piece. Smooth out all of the wrinkles, and pin the two pieces together along the edges. Place a few pins in the center of the quilt to hold it in place. Trim away any excess fabric on the sides.

Machine baste around all four edges of the blanket, removing pins as you go.

4. MACHINE QUILT BLANKET

Starting at the top right of the quilt, approximately $6''$ from the side edge, stitch a straight line from the top to the bottom of the blanket. Continue in this manner, moving from right to left, placing each row of stitching approximately $6''$ apart. To keep the quilt from becoming too cumbersome, roll up the stitched part of the quilt as you proceed.

5. ATTACH BINDING

Starting at one edge of the quilt, and using a 60″ length of bias tape, fold the short length of the bias tape over ½″ to cover the raw edge. Then place the fold of the bias tape over the edge of the blanket, thereby enclosing the raw edge of the blanket in the bias tape. Use a zigzag stitch to secure the bias binding to the blanket. Complete all four sides of the blanket, overlapping the bias tape at the corners.

6. FINISH BLANKET

To make the ties, fold in the short ends of the bias tape ½″ to cover the raw edge. Stitch along the entire edge of the bias tape to close the fold, ending with another ½″ fold at the end.

On any side of the quilt, measure in 8″ from the edge and place one end of each of the ties on top of each other along the edge of the quilt. Secure the ends to the outside of the blanket with a square stitch. The blanket can now be folded in half twice, rolled, and then tied.

the Family Heart

~~~~~~~~

S tepping away from the family home and out into the world on our own can be both exciting and nerve-racking—whether it's an extended business trip for papa or a first sleepover away from home for a little one. While there is much to look forward to, there is also a bit of vulnerability.

This Family Heart project was created as a small token of family, love, and connection that loved ones can carry with them as they leave the family to pursue their own adventures. With a little pocket for love notes, the stuffed Family Heart can be a wonderfully comforting and soft reminder of the family love we all carry with us—regardless of our physical space from one another.

Pattern Details

Beginner
A half-day project
Suitable for help from little hands
Finished size: 6″ in diameter

Use What You Have

Vintage quilt pieces are wonderful for this project, but any fabric will do; soft and comfortable are the most important criteria. For the pocket, wool sweater scraps are perfect, but any similarly weighted fabric will work just as well. *(The photographed heart is made from a vintage cutter quilt piece with a wool sweater scrap for the pocket.)*

Materials

Approximately ¼ yard total, as follows:

Fabric 1: (2) 9″ × 9″ pieces for the heart
Fabric 2: (1) 2½″ × 2½″ piece for the pocket
Stuffing
Pattern piece G (found on page 186)
Dried lavender: 1 tablespoon

1. PREPARE MATERIALS

Gather all materials and cut all fabrics to the measurements given above. Use pattern piece G to cut out two hearts from the 9″ × 9″ fabric.

2. ATTACH POCKET

Place the pocket square in the center of the front heart piece. Pin the square in place. Using a zigzag stitch, stitch around three sides of the square, leaving the top open for the pocket.

3. SEW HEART

Align the front and back heart pieces, right sides together. Pin the two pieces in place. Beginning on one side of the heart, stitch around the entire heart, stopping 2″ before your starting point.

Trim the point of the heart with scissors, being careful to avoid cutting the stitches. At the top V of the heart, trim the seam close to the stitching. Place notches around the curves, stopping the cuts just before the stitching.

Turn the heart right side out, and use a chopstick or a pencil to gently push out the points and curves. Press.

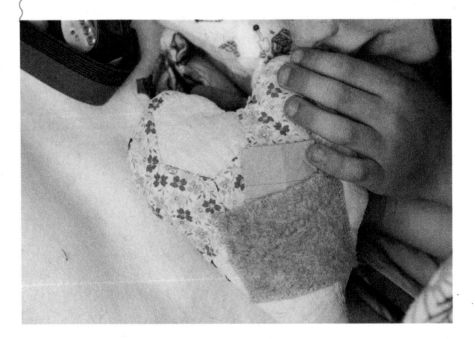

4. FINISH HEART

Through the 2″ opening on the side, stuff the heart lightly with the filling of your choice. Distribute the dried lavender inside as you go.

Hand-stitch the opening with a simple backstitch.

CRAFTY TIP

While readily available and affordable, most craft polyfills involve the use of chemicals, dyes, or bleach in their production. Fortunately, more and more ecologically sound alternatives are available. Raw wool (cleaned and carded) is a wonderful option and may be available from a local farm. Other nontoxic stuffing alternatives include loose organic cotton fiber. See www.organiccottonplus.com.

family sweater hats

~~~~~~~~~~

The sweater hat is one of my favorite quick and cozy sewing projects because it's made entirely from repurposed materials and solely for the purpose of keeping someone cozy and warm. Creating a sweater hat is one of my favorite ways to extend the life of a sweater and to keep my little ones warm during the cooler months of fall and winter. Completed with just a few seams, these comfy hats are the perfect project for days when you only have a few moments to create and want immediate results.

Pattern Details

Beginner
A half-day project
Finished size: Infant/toddler (child's medium, child's large/women's, men's)

Use What You Have

This project calls for the use of an adult-sized sweater, slightly felted. If the sweater is not already felted, you can do so by washing it by itself in hot soapy water. Wash the sweater repeatedly until it has properly shrunk and the knit fibers of the sweater are tight and close together. Felting will only work with sweaters that have a 90 to 100 percent wool content. (*Note:* Save the leftover sweater pieces to make the Fiber Garland on page 161.) *(The photographed projects are made from an old recycled wool sweater.)*

Materials

Fabric 1: (1) adult-sized or large child-sized sweater, made with 90 to 100 percent wool
Pattern pieces H, I, J, or K depending on size (found on pages 187–89)
Optional: Felt, wool, embroidery floss and needle, or buttons for embellishments

1. PREPARE PATTERN

Gather all materials. Lay the sweater flat on a cutting surface, making sure the front and back of the sweater are correctly aligned and free of wrinkles. Place the pattern piece on the bottom hem of the sweater. Pin the pattern in place. Cut around the pattern piece, through both the front and back of the sweater. Follow the instructions on the pattern piece for the desired size.

2. SHAPE CROWN

Transfer the bottom point of the V on the pattern piece to the front and back pieces of the hat by marking it with a pin. Fold each piece in half, right sides together, side to side. Make a mark 1″ from the center fold. Working with one piece at a time, stitch a straight line from the pin mark to the 1″ mark. Repeat this process with the second piece.

3. ADD EMBELLISHMENT

If your desired embellishments require sewing, do that now. Be sure to leave room close to the edge of your piece for a seam allowance.

4. FINISH HAT

Placing both pieces right sides together, stitch from one side of the hat across the top and down to the other side, stitching down the "flap" you created in step 2 as you go. Repeat the line of stitching ⅛" closer to the center of the hat.

Trim away the excess fabric. Clip the curves, being careful to avoid cutting the stitching. Turn the hat right side out.

Doily scarf

~~~~~~~~~

*O*oilies seem to be something I come across often, both as family heirlooms and when I'm out thrifting and antiquing. Unfortunately we have much less use for them in our homes today when compared to years past. Still, the handwork on doilies is some of the most beautiful and intricate of domestic arts, and finding alternative uses for them gives them a proper chance to be admired and used in a new way.

I used the combination of a lightweight wool, a vintage bedsheet fabric, and the lacey effects of doilies to give this project a light, airy feeling—just like the lacey, airy feeling that well-made doilies evoke in me. As an added delight, this project is a wonderful showcase for all the vintage buttons I adore!

Pattern Details

Intermediate
A half-day project
Finished size: 6″ × 62″

Use What You Have

One side of the main scarf panels can be made from wool, tweed, or suiting material; the other can be made from a lightweight fabric such as vintage bed-sheets, quilting cotton, or a tablecloth. *(The photographed scarf is made from six vintage and thrifted doily coasters, all on a lightweight wool blanket piece and backed with a vintage cotton bedsheet.)*

Materials

Approximately 2 yards total, as follows:

Fabric 1: (1) 6½″ × 63″ piece of wool for the scarf front
Fabric 2: (1) 6½″ × 63″ piece of cotton for the scarf back
Doilies: (4–6) no larger than 5″ diameter
Button: (4–6) of any size
Embroidery needle and floss

1. PREPARE MATERIALS

Gather all materials and cut all fabrics to the measurements given above.

2. PREPARE SCARF TOP

Working with the wool piece, place the doilies evenly across the length of scarf. Pin the doilies in place. Machine stitch the doily to the scarf piece by stitching ⅛″ in from the edges of the doily, keeping the fabric taut and flat as you go, to avoid puckering.

Using embroidery floss, sew a button to the center of each doily, tying off the floss on the wrong side of the wool fabric.

3. SEW SCARF

Lay the wool piece flat, with the buttons and right side facing up. On top of this, lay the cotton back, right side down. Both right sides are now facing each other. Smooth the cotton piece over the wool. Use pins along the sides every 4″–6″ to hold the pieces together.

Beginning in the middle of one long side of the scarf, begin to stitch a seam. Continue around all four sides of the scarf, stopping 4″ before you come to the original starting point and leaving an opening for turning the project right side out.

4. FINISH SCARF

Trim all four corners, being careful to avoid cutting too close to the stitching. Turn the scarf right side out through the opening. Use a chopstick or pencil to gently push out the four corners until they are distinct points.

Press. Stitch around the entire scarf, ¼″ from the edge, thereby closing up the opening of the scarf.

Adelaide's Pillowcase Dress

~~~~~~~~

*T*he classic pillowcase dress has been made by generations of mothers with various twists and tweaks on the style. The following pattern is based loosely on a vintage dress that I found at an estate sale. I added a little bit of my own tweaking to make it just right for my little one. I think this style has been around for ages because it's perfect in its simplicity, comfort, and resourcefulness. Easy to wear, perfect for the beach, and ideal for summer days spent playing outside, this dress keeps your little one cool and light in clothing so she can put her energy into the important work of playing.

Pattern Details

Intermediate
A half-day project
Finished size: 12–18 months (2T–3T, 4–5 years)

Use What You Have

Vintage pillowcases offer a wide diversity of styles and patterns. From the delicate embroidered linens of the 1940s to the flower power prints of the 1960s, there's sure to be a style that suits you and your little one. Pillowcases are easy to find at thrift shops and yard sales, and they are almost always inexpensive. The very lightweight, older embroidered cases are sometimes hard to work with and perhaps not best for your first dress. If you would like to make the dress as a top, simply follow a smaller size.

(The photographed dress is made from a vintage pillowcase.)

Materials

Approximately 1 yard total, as follows:

Fabric 1: (1) pillowcase (standard or king size)
Double-fold bias tape: (1) package (*Note:* You'll use approximately 100″.)
Pinking shears

1. PREPARE MATERIALS

Gather all materials. Begin by laying the pillowcase flat with the hemmed side (open edge) facing down. Measuring from the hem up 17″ (18″, 21″), mark and cut the pillowcase. You will be working with the bottom piece; toss the top piece in your scrap bag for a future project.

2. SHAPE DRESS TOP

Fold the pillowcase in half widthwise, keeping the open edge at the bottom. Keeping the pillowcase folded, use a piece of chalk or pencil to mark 12″ (13″, 17″) up from the bottom hem on both sides. Next, mark the top center with a pin. Draw a gradual curve from each pencil point to the top pin. Using the curved lines and the three points as your guide, cut through all four layers of the folded pillowcase to create a point at the center top.

3. PLEAT DRESS TOP

Open up the folded pillowcase. Working with the center U shape on the front of the pillowcase only (the dress center, top, front) place one pin in at the bottom of the U, another evenly between this pin and the point, and a second at the same place on the other side of the U. Repeat the process on the back.

Create an inverted box pleat at each pin. Starting ½″ from the pin, fold the fabric over on itself toward the pin. The fold will be ¼″. Press. Repeat the fold on the other side of pin, bringing the fabric toward the pin once again. Press and pin both pleats in place. This completes one box pleat. Repeat this process at each pin for a total of six box pleats.

Stitch the top of the pleats ¼″ from the edge to hold them in place. Remove the pins as you go.

For sizes 12 months and 2T–3T, place one more additional box pleat at each underarm seam. Stitch the pleats as instructed above, and as seen in the photograph.

4. CREATE BIAS BINDING

Pin the bias tape to the front center (where the pleats were just applied), fold the bias over the edge of the fabric, and then use a zigzag stitch to hold the bias in place. This process will enclose the raw edge of the fabric in the binding. Repeat the same process for the back center and the underarm binding. Set the dress aside.

5. FINISH DRESS

To create the shoulder ties, cut four lengths of bias tape to 12″ and sew the binding closed using a zigzag stitch. (See step 8 on page 54 for help on keeping the small fabric point from slipping into your machine.)

Attach one shoulder tie to the dress at each point on the front side, placing the ties ¼″ below the point. Secure the ties with a zigzag stitch. Place the remaining two ties on the back points following the same procedure.

On the tying end of the tie, make a simple knot, approximately 1″ in from the end. Trim away any excess tie with pinking shears.

By the Seashore

And forget not that the earth delights to feel
your bare feet and the winds long to play with your hair.

—Kahlil Gibran

There is no denying that I am a homebody at heart. My interests, heart, and soul are right in the center of my home. And yet, there is nothing like a little adventure or a brief outing to fill my soul with new ideas, inspiration, energy, and joy. More often than not, for our family in particular, we head to the water. Rivers, lakes, ponds, streams, and our beloved ocean—all of them are treasured and loved by each and every one of us.

Sometimes we walk on our favorite river trail, where my children know all the turns and bends in the path. Other times, we put our canoe in a new lake we've discovered and just drift and see what the water is like and what creatures live there. Occasionally, I find time for a rare and treasured date at the beach with my love or a summer evening with girlfriends, sitting on a dock, eating watermelon, and watching the flow of the river—and the worries of our days—float on by on their way to the wide ocean.

Living in the Northeast, we are ever aware of the changing of our seasons. In the summer—my favorite time of year—the beach bag is perpetually packed, summer adventures are planned, and days are spent outside from waking until bedtime. The blissful memories and feelings of summer are ones we carry with us all year round. In the autumn, we soak up the last bits of sun before a long winter ahead. It's a season of lingering in the sun and the falling leaves, and preparing for what is to come. In the winter we find beauty and inspiration in the crispness of the white, white world around us, treasuring each small moment as we breathe the fresh, cold air. And in the spring, our adventures are full of promise and hope at the unearthing of the new life we find in the natural world.

Whether it be watching and listening for birds in the woods, catching waves in the ocean, climbing a tree in the park, building a snow fort in our yard, or bearing witness to a magical show of nature and its creatures, I treasure these family adventures. Our family of five experiences very few moments when we are all still at the very same time—and yet, we find it happens most outside when we are engaged, together, and in awe of the magic and beauty we see before our eyes. It's in these moments that I find us all so very present—hearts healthily pumping and each of us fully aware and completely alive.

Nearly as lovely as the time spent outside are the treasures we bring back inside with us. The outside world seems to bring such clarity to all of the priorities, ideas, and big and little decisions that we make in our lives. Even when our time outside has been spent wild and active, we return home to our inside lives feeling more calm, centered, and connected. Our home becomes stronger, clearer, and more comforting for having spent some time away.

In nature, we find so many things. At the water's edge, atop a mountain, or in the middle of a park, I watch my children flourish in who they are. With all the distractions, toys, and walls out of the way, the essence of who they are just shines. When I remember to pay attention, I see it radiating so strongly that I can't help but be brought right into it myself. My children are experts on breathing, on living; they know how to do it. And the open air? Why, that's breath itself. When I find myself in the midst of unsettling chaos—full of more commitments and expectations than we can really handle— I need to look no further than my little ones for the answer to what I've forgotten: Stop. Breathe. Listen. Then we head straight to the beach, or right to the woods, and play until we find ourselves restored.

The great outdoors holds so much magic for you to witness and experience together as a family. The woods, the ocean, the mountains ... They're calling to you. Can you hear them? Go ahead; go gather your little ones, and go play.

5

Retreat

Projects to inspire calm and peace

~~~~~~~~~~~~~~~~~~~~~

The patterns and projects in Retreat are intended to inspire calm and peace. These projects contribute to a warm
home environment and are suitable for any number of
home-based activities—from relaxing as a family to dreaming at night alone.

quilt strip pillow

~~~~~~~~

This project was inspired by a bundle of vintage quilt strips I found at a flea market one day. I always consider myself lucky to stumble upon old quilt pieces like these works in progress from years past. I wonder who made them, how the project began, and of course, why it was stopped before it was finished. Was the quilter too busy? Did she lose interest in the design? I'd like to think that the original maker would be pleased to know that years later her project was indeed picked up and finished by someone else who loved the pieces dearly.

This pillow showcases much-loved fabrics, and made as a cover to a pillow form, it's also washable—an essential for any family!

Pattern Details

Intermediate
A half-day project
Finished size: 19″ × 19″

Use What You Have

This pillow pattern is a wonderful use of vintage bedspreads as a fabric for the base. I particularly love the feel and look of vintage matelasse bedspreads. They have a thickness, and yet with their vintage wear, they also have a softness that is hard to replicate in modern fabrics.

This pillow is a great way to salvage a piece of a bedspread that might contain stains and tears. The strips on the front of the pillow can be vintage quilt strips or simply any strips of fabric, making them a wonderful use of scraps. (*The photographed pillow is made from a vintage matelasse bedspread for the base with found quilt strips on top. The second pillow photographed includes a vintage redwork embroidery pattern found at www.patternbee.com.*)

Materials

Approximately 1 1/2 yards total, as follows:

Fabric 1: (1) 19″ × 19″ piece for the front
Fabric 2: (4) 2″ × 19″ strips for the front
Fabric 3: (2) 13″ × 19″ pieces for the back
Pillow form: (1) 18 ″ × 18″

1. PREPARE MATERIALS

Gather all materials and cut all fabrics to the measurements above.

2. MAKE PILLOW TOP

Begin by preparing the strips for the front of the pillow. If you are using strips of fabric and would like a fringed, raw edge, tear the strips of fabric in the direction of the fabric's grain. (*Note:* You may need to snip the fabric with scissors at the beginning to get the tear started.) Cut the fabric into 19″ lengths.

Arrange these strips of fabric on the pillow front piece (19″ × 19″) as desired, and pin them in place.

Stitch along both sides of the fabric strips ¼″ from the edge, securing the strips to the pillow front. Put the pillow front aside.

3. PREPARE BACK FABRIC

On one of the 19″ edges on one back fabric piece, fold the fabric over toward the wrong side ¼″. Press. Fold over again ½″. Press, and pin the fold in place. Stitch close to folded edge along the length of the fold. (*Note:* Decorative stitches work well here. Most machines have at least a zigzag stitch, if not more options.) Repeat this process on the second back piece.

4. FINISH PILLOW

Lay your front fabric piece flat on a surface, right side up. On top of this, lay one of the back pieces, right side facing down. Align it with the top half of the pillow front so the hemmed edge of the back fabric piece is in the center of the pillow front. On top of that, lay the second back piece right side down, aligning it with the bottom half of the pillow front, again so the hemmed edge of the back fabric piece is in the center of the pillow front. The two back pieces will overlap in the center. Pin the pieces in place.

Stitch around all four sides of the pillow, securing the fabric where it overlaps by backstitching. Trim the corners. Turn the pillowcase inside out. Place the pillow form inside the case.

Remove the pillow form from the pillowcase to hand-wash the case.

EARTHY TIP

Consider using a greener alternative to the traditional craft pillow forms. Nature-Fil makes a bamboo pillow form insert, which can be found in some shops and online at www.hartsfabrics .com.

one-word banner

~~~~~~~~~~

*E*arly in our family life, before my first son's second birthday, I threw together a quick happy birthday banner made out of fabric. I had no idea how important that banner would become in our family's traditions and our year-to-year celebrations of birthdays. My little ones have never forgotten that banner as they prepare for the birthday of a sibling. To date, our birthday banner has hung at birthday parties from a medieval birthday party in our dining room to a midlake ice birthday party deep in the northern Maine woods. It isn't a birthday at our house without the birthday banner.

Fortunately, you don't need a special occasion, like a holiday or a birthday to make such a banner for your home. Sometimes just one little word or phrase can evoke such positive change in the course of our day to inspire, comfort, or encourage us as a family. Perhaps there's a word—a family motto—that resonates with your family. Or perhaps you'd like to incorporate a word into your family's life. Whatever your purpose, a message banner can be a wonderful, constant, and beautiful visual reminder of those qualities that are important to us as a family.

Pattern Details

Intermediate
A day project
Finished size: Several feet, depending on the word length

Use What You Have

The materials needed for this banner are most likely lying around as scraps. Wool blanket pieces work wonderfully as the flags for the banners, and you only need a few scraps of fabric to create the letters. Don't limit yourself to just letters; symbols are just as meaningful. *(The photographed banner is made from a vintage wool blanket and scrap fabric pieces.)*

Materials

Approximately 2 yards total, as follows:

Fabric 1: (1) 6″ × 14″ piece of wool for each flag, approximately 2 yards total
Fabric 2: (1) 4″ × 5″ piece of scrap fabric for each letter
Fabric marker or chalk
Length of ribbon, bias tape, or twine (*Note:* I used 48″ of binding for the five-letter word pictured in this project.)

1. PREPARE MATERIALS

Gather all materials and cut all fabrics to the measurements given above.

2. CUT OUT LETTERS

To create the fabric letters freehand: Write the outline of the letter directly on the fabric with chalk or a fabric marker. Cut the fabric following the marker lines. Small scissors are useful for this part of the project.

To create uniform letters: Print letters from any word processing program, enlarging the letters so that the tallest letter is no bigger than $4\frac{1}{2}''$. Cut out the letters. Place the paper letters over the fabric scrap squares and trace them with the marker or chalk. Cut the fabric following the marker lines. Small scissors are useful for this part of the project.

3. SEW LETTERS TO FLAGS

Place the fabric letter on the wool squares, aligning them in the center from left to right and $1''$ up from the bottom of one of the $6''$ sides. Pin the letters in place. Repeat this process for all of letters.

Machine stitch the letters to the wool squares, approximately $\frac{1}{8}''$ from the edge of the fabric. The stitching will leave a raw edge on the fabric with just the slightest room for some natural fraying.

SOME WORDS TO GET YOU THINKING

dream	together
create	home
play	grow
laugh	escape
nourish	breathe
love	hope
life	spring
live	summer
joy	autumn
peace	winter
shine	

4. FINISH BANNER

Lay the binding (ribbon or twine) flat on a large surface. Place the banner squares where you would like them to be on the binding. Leave approximately 6″ at each end to tie the banner. Pin the squares over the binding and stitch them in place.

Hang the banner where desired. Hooks and drawer knobs make decorative hangers.

Fiber Garland

~~~~~~~~

I remember the colorful plastic beads—hippie beads, we called them—that once hung from my childhood bedroom doorway, hand-me-downs from my mother's own childhood in the 1960s. I loved those beads, and I thought I'd like to make some with and for my little ones—with our own green, more natural, recycled spin, of course!

With three little ones of different ages—yet all relatively young—it can be challenging to find craft projects that are fun, safe, and successful for everyone. This Fiber Garland might just be the best we've found yet.

I first introduced this project to my children on a cold and wet fall afternoon, when we had been inside for days waiting out the weather. Emptying a basket of wool sweater pieces, felt bits, and other fabrics onto the middle of a table, I handed each child a pair of scissors and told them to get cutting. They were thrilled. How could they not be with a big pile of fabric and no rules besides cutting it all up into pieces! Highly satisfying and highly rewarding, our pile of cut fabric pieces grew higher and higher as we dreamed up all the many places our soon-to-be-garland could be strung.

Pattern Details

Beginner
A half-day project
Suitable for little hands
Finished size: 1″ squares of wool (or other size of
  your choosing) strung to any length you like

Use What You Have

Any and all kinds of wool work well for this project, including old sweaters, felt, wool blazers, coats, and so on. You'll likely want to felt the wool before beginning by washing it in hot soapy water so that the fibers shrink a bit closer together. *(The photographed garlands are made entirely from recycled, felted sweaters from our own closets.)*

Materials

Fabric: Scraps of wool
Thick thread for stringing the garland
Heavy-duty hand-sewing needle
Wood, glass, or plastic beads

I. PREPARE MATERIALS

Gather all materials. Cut the wool pieces into approximately 1″ squares. The squares do not need to be precise, so this step is an excellent way to include children of all ages. The shapes needn't be exclusively square, either. Triangles, circles, free-form shapes of all kinds will work. Let your children lead the way on this one!

2. ASSEMBLE GARLAND

Choose the desired length for your garland. Double this number and add 10″. Cut the thread to this length.

Thread the needle, doubling your strand of thread, tying a knot at the end. Add the wool pieces and beads as you desire.

When the garland is complete, tie another knot at the end to secure the pieces.

3. FINISH GARLAND

Hang the garland from a doorway, bunk beds, a ceiling, or a curtain rod.

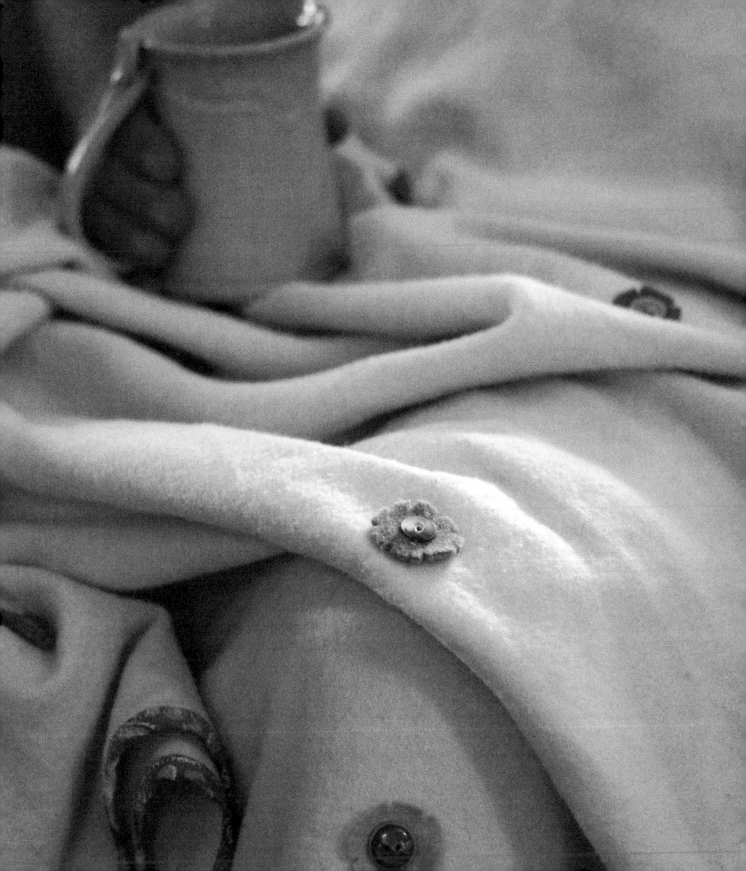

button flower blanket

During our cool Maine winters (and even during our cool Maine summers!), blankets are always in high demand—in every room, and by every family member, all the time. This blanket came together as one more blanket to keep off the chill.

As I pick up wool blankets while thrifting, I'll often find a perfectly usable blanket that is partially stained or damaged. This fact usually makes an otherwise expensive find quite affordable, and by cutting off the damaged part of the blanket, I can salvage what's left into a new and improved version of its former self.

This project provides a way to save a perfectly lovely piece of wool, while adding some fun elements of buttons and felt that not only serve as decorative elements, but also as creative cover-ups for any tiny stains that may be left on the piece.

Pattern Details

Intermediate
A weekend project
Finished size: 58″ × 46″

Use What You Have

Wool blankets—or a large piece of wool fabric—are best for this project. Wool scraps from sweaters, felt, or the Fiber Garland project on page 161 are perfect for the wool circles. *(The photographed blanket is made from a vintage wool blanket, recycled wool sweater scraps, vintage buttons, and vintage fabric binding.)*

Materials

Approximately 3 yards total, as follows:

Fabric 1: (1) 58″ × 46″ piece of wool
Fabric 2: (25) wool circles 1″ diameter
Buttons: (25) no bigger than ½″ each
Embroidery needle and floss in coordinating button color
Extra-wide double-fold bias tape: 250″ long

I. PREPARE MATERIALS

Gather all materials and cut all fabrics to the measurements given above.

2. ATTACH WOOL CIRCLES AND BUTTONS

Begin by preparing the wool circles. Using sharp scissors, cut a V into a wool circle with the point of the V approximately ¼" from the edge of circle. Repeat this cut five or six times evenly around the circle. Continue until you have made 25 wool circles.

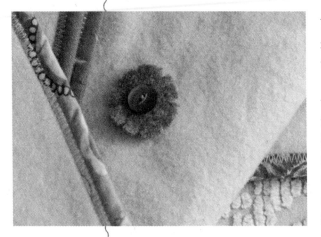

Distribute the circles as desired on the blanket, allowing yourself at least 2" of room on all four edges of the blanket. Pin the circles in place.

Place a button at the center of one wool circle, and pull up embroidery floss from behind, leaving a 2" tail to tie later (do not knot). Hold this tail in place as you secure the button and the wool circle to the blanket. Finish by tying a simple knot on the back side. Trim the floss to ¼". Repeat this process for each circle and its corresponding button.

3. ATTACH BINDING AND FINISH BLANKET

Attach bias tape to the blanket by starting at a corner. Fold the bias tape around the blanket edge, and stitch a wide zigzag stitch, overlapping the edge of the binding and the blanket (on the front and back) for the entire length of that edge. Trim the bias at the next corner.

To begin at the second corner, allow ½" of the bias to extend beyond the corner. Fold this piece, with the tape open, over the backside of the

CRAFTY TIP

As an alternative to buying bias tape, it's easy to make your own binding, which will also use up and show off some smaller pieces of fabric. To make your own bias binding, you'll need a bias binding maker, which comes in a variety of sizes depending on the size binding you want. Instructions are included in the packaging.

corner, and then fold the binding onto the back side to attach it as you did previously. In this way, you've covered the corner with bias.

Continue applying the bias to the remaining sides. At the end of the last side, repeat the same wrapping to cover the corner where you began stitching.

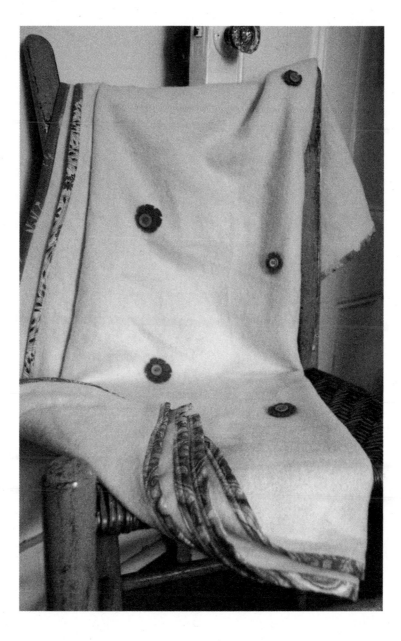

Handkerchief curtain

~~~~~~~~~~

I was recently given a collection of my grandmother's beautiful handkerchiefs. Many of them became part of our regular household use (as an alternative to tissues), but some of them were just too pretty and special to use for such practical purposes. I wanted to really see the beautiful fabrics on some of these treasures, and I thought this curtain might be just the right romantic, dreamy creation to do so.

This curtain works well in any place where you'd like a bit of privacy or a decorative touch but still want to allow as much light as possible to come in.

Pattern Details

Intermediate
A day project
Finished size: As needed to fit your window

Use What You Have

This project is perfect for your inherited collection of grandma's handkerchiefs! In addition to thrifting, you can often find many handkerchiefs at online auction sites, where groups of them are sold by color. White bed sheeting no longer in use is an excellent base for the curtain panel. Cotton fabric works well as a replacement. *(The photographed curtain is made from a thrifted vintage bedsheet and handkerchiefs from my grandmother's collection.)*

Materials

Approximately 2 yards total, depending on window size, as follows:

Fabric 1: White cotton as determined in steps 1 and 2
Fabric 2: (4–8) pressed handkerchiefs
Embroidered ribbon: (6) 8″ long
Tension rod to fit the window

I. DETERMINE SIZE OF CURTAIN

Width: Measure the width of your window on the inside recess. Multiply this number by two. This measurement is your fabric width.

Length: Measure the length from the top of the rod (put the rod in position to measure) to ½″ above the sill (or as desired). Add 5″ to this number. This measurement is your fabric length.

2. PREPARE MATERIALS

Gather all materials and cut all fabrics to the measurements determined in step 1.

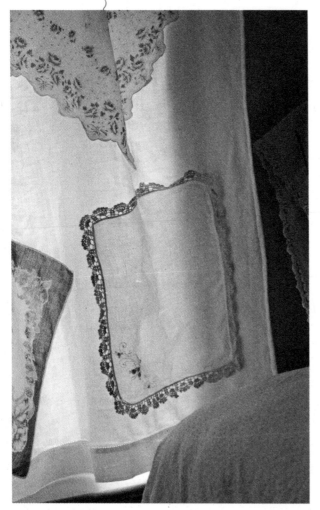

3. HEM CURTAIN

Fold one side edge of the cotton fabric piece toward the wrong side of the fabric ½″. Press. Repeat, folding again 1″. Press. Stitch. Repeat this process on the opposite side.

On the bottom, fold the fabric toward the wrong side ½″. Press. Fold again 2″. Press. Stitch. Repeat this process at the top edge of the curtain.

4. ATTACH HANDKERCHIEFS

Lay the cotton panel on a flat surface and arrange the handkerchiefs in a pattern of your choosing. Pin each one securely in place.

Stitch each handkerchief to the panel, working ¼″ from the edge on all four sides.

5. ATTACH RIBBON

On the top edge of the curtain panel, and beginning 1″ in from the side edge, evenly space six pins across the top edge. (*Note:* If the curtain is particularly wide, you'll want to add a few more pins and embroidered loops in this step.)

Take an embroidered ribbon, and fold and press each end ½" toward the wrong side. Then, fold the entire ribbon in half, creating a loop with the fold at the top. Place this loop on the wrong side of fabric at the first pinned mark, matching the raw edges of the loop with the edge stitching 2" down from the top. Pin the embroidered ribbon loop in place. Repeat this process for all of the ribbons and the pinned marks.

6. FINISH CURTAIN

Create a box pleat around each ribbon base by folding ½" of the fabric to each side of the ribbon over to cover the ribbon loop in the back. Press, and pin the pleats in place.

Stitch each pleat in place by sewing a square: stitch across the top edge of curtain panel, down one side of the pleat, across the stitching on the bottom of the top hem, and back up the other side of the pleat. This square will secure the ribbon and the box pleat in place.

Slide a tension rod through the ribbon loops and hang the curtain in a window.

memory tree quilt art

~~~~~~~~~~

I'm sure I'm not the only mama who gets a little sentimental about the clothing my little ones wore in their infancy. And while most of our outgrown clothing ends up at our local clothing swap, or in the hands of friends and family, I always save a few bits just for us. Those pieces evoke so much emotion and so many memories that I just can't bear to part with them. I tuck away special pieces—perhaps for the grandchildren—and then there are the rest. The sentimental pieces that don't get turned into other projects become a work of art. Make this wonderful project with your little ones, as you tell the tales and the memories associated with each piece of fabric from "when they were little."

Pattern Details

Intermediate
A weekend
Finished size: 15″ × 15″

Use What You Have

Your children's outgrown clothing is ideal for this project. Almost all types of fabrics will work well—knits included. The base of the quilt is suitable for a number of different fabrics—linen, quilt pieces, cotton, bedspread materials, and so forth. *(The photographed art is made from Ezra's baby clothes on a base of linen.)*

Materials

Approximately 1 yard total, as follows:

Fabric 1: (9) 4″ × 3″ pieces of fabric cut from clothing
Fabric 2: (1) 8½″ × 11″ piece of tree-colored fabric
Fabric 3: (2) 15″ × 15″ pieces of fabric for the base
Heat'n Bond Lite Iron-On Adhesive: (1) 8½″ × 11″ piece, (9) 4″ × 3″ pieces
Quilt batting: (1) 15″ × 15″
Embroidery needle and floss
Embroidery hoop
Extra-wide bias tape: (1) 70″ long
Pattern pieces L, M, and N (found on page 190–91)
Choose one display option:

For dowel rod display—¼″ × 17″ dowel, (1) 14″ length of extra-wide bias tape, ribbon
For framing display—16″ × 16″ frame, 16″ × 16″ acid-free art board for mounting, double-sided tape

1. PREPARE MATERIALS

Gather all materials and cut all fabrics and adhesive to the measurements given above.

2. PREPARE FABRIC

Following the manufacturer's instructions for heat settings, attach the adhesive to the wrong side of all pieces of fabric, keeping the paper backing attached to the adhesive for now.

3. ATTACH TREE APPLIQUÉ

Trace pattern piece L on the wrong side of the $8\frac{1}{2}'' \times 11''$ fabric piece (on the paper backing). Cut out the tree, and peel off the paper backing. With one piece of the base fabric ($15'' \times 15''$) lying flat, right side up, position the tree at the bottom center and attach it following the adhesive instructions.

Machine stitch the tree to the base, $\frac{1}{8}''$ from the outline of the tree.

4. ATTACH LEAVES APPLIQUÉ

On the wrong side of each $4'' \times 3''$ clothing piece (on the paper backing), trace one copy of pattern piece M and one copy of pattern piece N (large and small leaves). Cut out the leaves, and place them in position around the tree trunk as desired. Pin the leaves in place. When all of the pieces are in place, remove the backing one at a time and attach the leaves following the manufacture's instructions.

5. EMBELLISH QUILT

If desired, embroider your child's name, birth date, or a special word on the quilt, using an embroidery hoop to keep the fabric taut as you go. Set the quilt top aside.

6. ASSEMBLE QUILT

Lay the second 15" × 15" square fabric piece for the quilt back wrong side up on a flat surface. On top of this piece, evenly place the quilt batting, followed by the finished quilt top, right side up. Pin the pieces in place. Machine baste around all four sides close to the edge.

7. QUILT LEAVES

Using three strands of embroidery floss and a running stitch, embroider each of the leaves. You can do this as either an outline around the entire leaf or a line straight down the center of the leaf, making a vein, or as a combination of both techniques.

8. ATTACH BINDING

Attach bias tape to the front side of the quilt by starting in the center of one side of the quilt, leaving 4" free to join the ends later. Place the raw edge of the open bias along the raw edge of the quilt. Stitch the binding to the quilt along the fold of the bias tape, stopping ½" before the first corner. Backstitch. Trim the threads.

Fold the long end of bias binding away from the blanket, making a 90-degree angle with the binding side you just attached. Then, fold the binding back toward the unbound side of the blanket, readying it for the second side. Keep the fold of the bias on the corner aligned with the binding attached on the first side. Pin the bias in place.

Beginning on this second side, ½″ in from the corner, continue stitching along the second side as you did with the first. Repeat the process on the corners and the sides, stopping about 4″ from the beginning of the binding.

Unfold both unstitched ends of the bias binding. Lay the two ends of the binding flat on top of each other. On the top piece of binding, use tailor's chalk to mark a 45-degree angle where the two pieces meet. On the piece below, mark another line, ½″ beyond the first chalk mark to allow for a seam.

Trim the strips along the marked lines. With the right sides together, stitch the ends of these strips together. Press the seam open. Refold the binding as it was before, trimming the points as needed. Attach this binding to the quilt as you did on the other sides.

9. FINISH QUILT

To finish the binding, fold it over the raw edge so the binding is toward the back side of the quilt. Pin the binding in place all the way around. Stitch the entire binding in place by sliding the needle up through the quilt, picking up a few threads of the binding's folded edge, and then sliding the needle back down through the quilt.

10. PREPARE FOR DISPLAY

Dowel rod display option: On the back side of the quilt, open up and pin the length of binding in place, 1" down from the top and centered across the middle. Hand-stitch down both lengths of the bias binding close to the binding's edge, going through the back layer and batting only so the stitching isn't visible on the front. Slide a dowel through the binding. Attach the ribbon to the ends of the dowel and hang the quilt.

Framing display option: Mount the quilt with double-sided mounting tape onto a 16" × 16" piece of acid-free art board (rag board). Frame and hang the quilt.

Comfortably Worn

Home is where we tie one end of the thread of life.
—Martin Buxbaum

The actual differences among our homes may be many. Your style may be modern or shabby chic; you may keep a tidy home or love your clutter; you may live in an apartment in the city or in a rambling farmhouse in the country. These specifics of our homes are as varied as we are, but I do believe something connects them all: they have soul. These items in our homes, and our homes in general, are in some way a reflection of ourselves and our lives, a connection to our past, a dream for our future. In other words, they have *life* to them.

I spend a lot of time not only making and looking for the things my family needs, but also looking for special pieces that have a sense of life in them. Wandering through the aisles of the forgotten, the old, and the thrown away at flea markets, thrift shops, and estate sales, I find many old bits with varied pasts and undetermined futures. I think a lot about where these things have come from and what they could be. We're fortunate to still have so many of these inspiring items around us. Whether they've been thrifted, found in our homes, or handed down from past generations, we're lucky to have them, not only as they are, but also as usable material and as inspiration to make something new.

Our house is full of old things; some are of the antique variety, and some are just old. When I look around any room in our home, I see so few things that are actually new. To some this may sound lovely and idealistic; to others this may sound dreadful. For us, surrounding ourselves with used stuff feels

PATCHWORK FURNITURE

My favorite way to spruce up an old, loved, and worn piece of furniture is to embellish it with something new. Doilies, pieces of fabric, and handwork pieces all make great patches on a chair, which then truly becomes a family work of art in the process. You'll want to use a heavy-duty hand-sewing needle—often found in the upholstery section of a craft store—for stitching embellishments onto furniture or upholstery. In addition, you'll want a hand-quilting cotton thread, which will give you a bit of extra strength as you tack your piece down to the fabric on a chair.

just right. However, a fine line exists between "old but worn just enough to live with it" and "just plain old and falling apart." Usually, I look around my home and see things that are comfortably worn, but on some days, when I face a lot of challenges or when I look at far too many magazine photos, it's the latter. I find myself constantly trying to keep my love for things and my desire for style in check with my consumer ethics, my value on the past, the resources that are readily available to us, and our attempts at the frugal and simplistic lifestyle we've chosen. Like everything else, it's a balance.

When I do have doubts, and when I'm very tempted to run to my nearest furniture store for an easy, new solution, I'm stopped and comforted by the stories that surround me and the life and energy and history that radiate from the furnishings in our home. Whether I actually know the stories doesn't matter. I can easily imagine the past life of a tattered vintage children's book or my great grandmother's dining table. More often than not, I feel blessed and quite rich, I dare say, to have them in my home. The life that emanates from these things, the stories they tell—real or imagined—comfort me.

Pattern Templates

Enlarge the patterns as instructed. If no enlargement is required, cut out shapes from the book or use tracing paper to create your own paper pattern. Be sure to transfer all markings and instructions from the pattern piece. PDFs of these patterns are also available to download at www.shambhala.com/HandmadeHome and www.amandasoule.com.

You are free to photocopy patterns from this book to make items for your personal use.

Broadturn Bag   Page **27**

Actual size

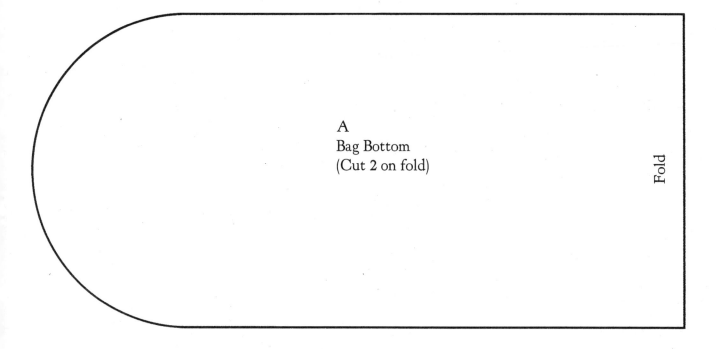

A
Bag Bottom
(Cut 2 on fold)

Fold

Actual size

B
Front Middle
(Cut 1)

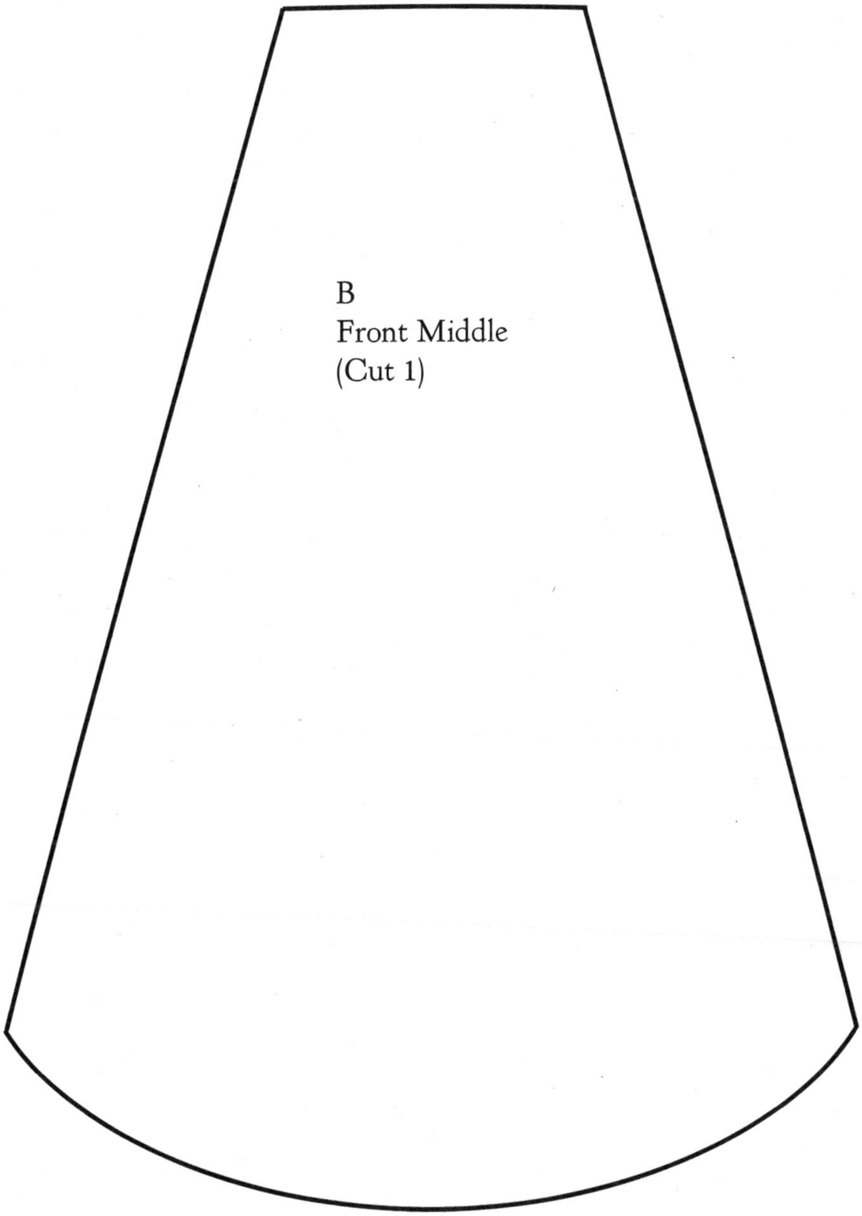

Millie's Hot Pad   Page 31

Actual size

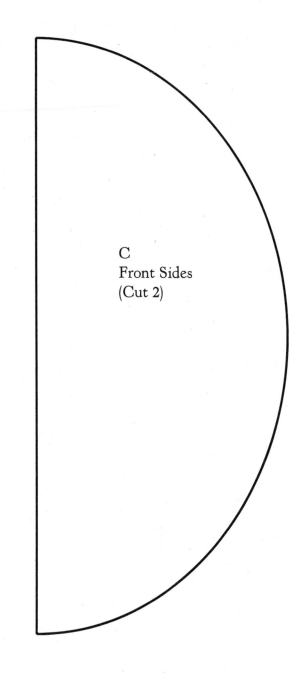

C
Front Sides
(Cut 2)

Actual size

D
Back
(Cut 1 from fabric;
Cut 2 from batting)

Actual size

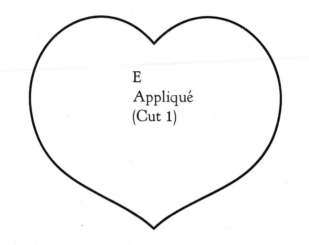

E
Appliqué
(Cut 1)

Shown at 50%; enlarge by 200%.

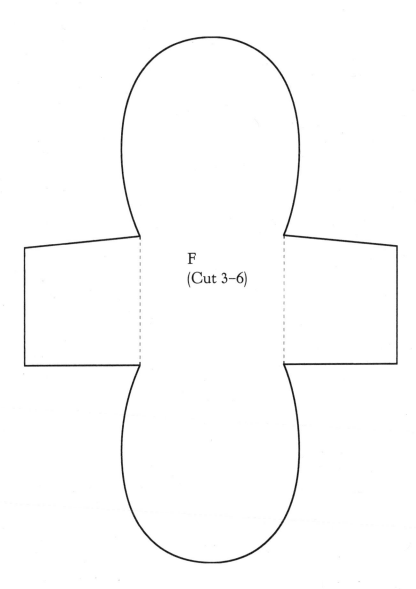

F
(Cut 3–6)

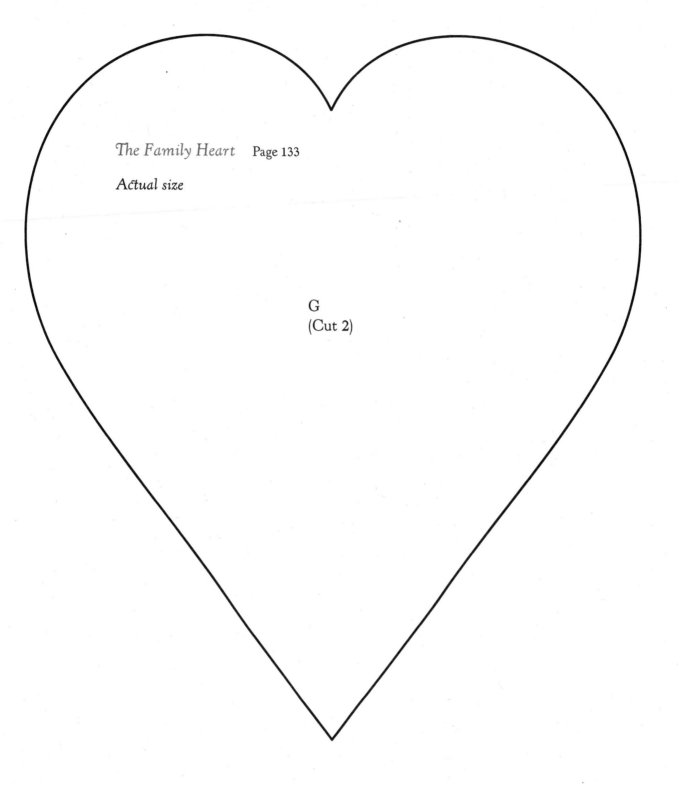

The Family Heart   Page 133

Actual size

G
(Cut 2)

Actual size

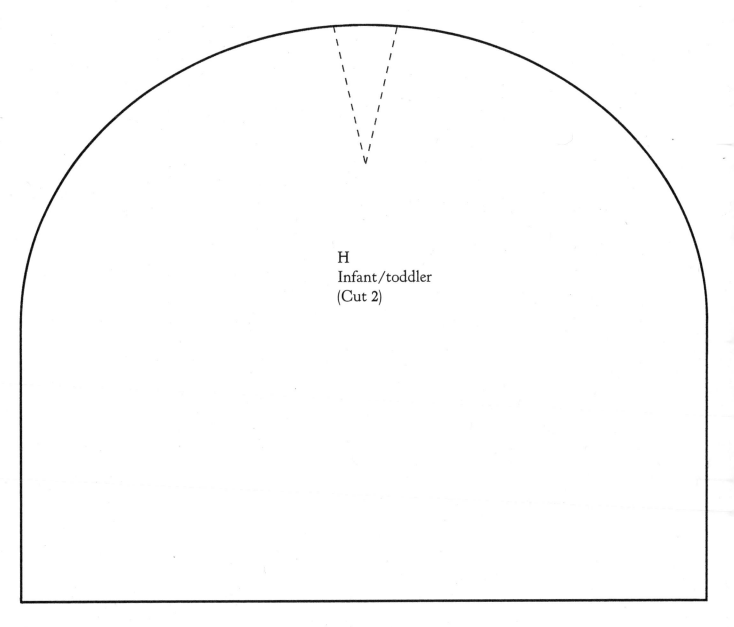

H
Infant/toddler
(Cut 2)

Shown at 50%; enlarge by 200%.

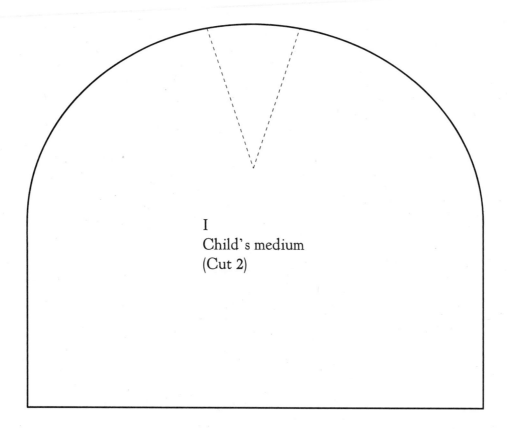

I
Child's medium
(Cut 2)

Shown at 50%; enlarge by 200%.

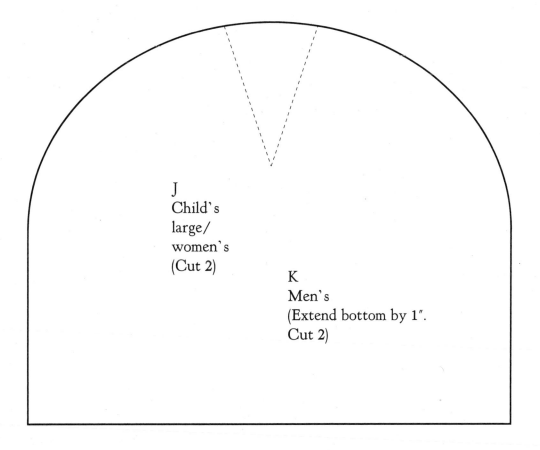

J
Child's
large/
women's
(Cut 2)

K
Men's
(Extend bottom by 1".
Cut 2)

Shown at 50%; enlarge by 200%.

L
Tree
appliqué
(Cut 1)

Actual size

M
Leaf
appliqué
(Cut 9)

N
Leaf
appliqué
(Cut 9)

Resources

Cloth Diapering and Organic Baby and Child Products

www.diaperjungle.com
www.diaperpin.com
www.mothering.com
www.realdiaperassociation.org
www.thebabywearer.com

Crafts Mentioned in This Book

Cannon, John, and Cannon, Margaret. *Dye Plants and Dyeing*. London: A & C Black Publishers, 2003.

Rudkin, Linda. *Natural Dyes*. London: A & C Black Publishers, 2007.

Smith, Esther. *How to Make Books: Fold, Cut & Stitch Your Way to a One-of-a-Kind Book*. New York: Potter Craft, 2007.

Sturges, Norma. *The Braided Rug Book: Creating Your Own American Folk Art*. Asheville, N.C.: Lark Books, 2006.

Friends and Neighbors Featured in this Book

www.broadturnfarm.com
www.pixiegenne.typepad.com

How-to-Sew Resources

www.craftster.org

Davis, Tina. *See & Sew: A Sewing Book for Children*. New York: Stuart, Tabori and Chang, 2006.

Karol, Amy. *Bend-the-Rules Sewing: The Essential Guide to a Whole New Way to Sew*. New York: Potter Craft, 2007.

Simplicity's *Simply the Best Sewing Book*. New York: Perennial Library, 1988.

Organic and Natural Sewing Supplies

http://americanhemptwine.com
www.earthfriendlygoods.com
www.envirotextile.com
www.heartofvermont.com
www.nearseanaturals.com
www.organiccottonplus.com
www.pmorganics.com
www.vreseis.com

Resourceful Family Living

Goldsmith, Sheherazade. *A Slice of Organic Life*. New York: DK Publishing, 2007.

O'Mara, Peggy. *Natural Family Living: The Mothering Magazine Guide to Parenting*. Memphis, Tenn.: Atria, 2000.

Siegel-Meier, Karyn. *Naturally Clean Home: 100 Safe and Easy Herbal Formulas for Nontoxic Cleansers.* North Adams, Mass.: Storey Publishing, 1999.

Trask, Crissy. *It's Easy Being Green.* Layton, Utah: Gibbs Smith, 2006.

Sustainable Food

www.csacenter.org
www.localharvest.org
slowfoodusa.org

Reusing and Recycling

www.craigslist.org
http://earth911.org
www.fleamarketguide.com
www.freecycle.org
www.greendisk.com
www.isharestuff.org

Green Home Improvement

www.buildinggreen.com
www.milkpaint.com
www.salvageweb.com